Industriebau –
Kontinuität im Wandel
Märker Zementwerk Harburg
Architekten
Ackermann und Partner

Industrial Architecture –
Continuity and Change
Märker Cement Works Harburg
Architekten
Ackermann und Partner

Industriebau –
Kontinuität im Wandel
Märker Zementwerk Harburg
Architekten
Ackermann und Partner

Industrial Architecture –
Continuity and Change
Märker Cement Works Harburg
Architekten
Ackermann und Partner

Wolfgang Jean Stock

Industriebau –
Kontinuität im Wandel
Märker Zementwerk Harburg
Architekten
Ackermann und Partner

Industrial Architecture –
Continuity and Change
Märker Cement Works Harburg
Architekten
Ackermann und Partner

Prestel München · London · New York

Durchbruch zur Industriekultur
Das Märker Zementwerk
der Architekten Ackermann und Partner

Eine Rede geht seit einigen Jahren um in Europa, die Rede
von der ›Informationsgesellschaft‹. Doch so häufig auch
von der zunehmenden Entmaterialisierung aller Lebensvor-
gänge gesprochen wird – Tatsache ist, dass selbst die
hoch entwickelten Gesellschaften für absehbare Zeit fort-
fahren werden, den Großteil ihrer Produktion auf industriel-
ler Grundlage zu leisten. Die ›Old Economy‹ wird weit weniger schnell veralten als es Trendforscher weissagen. Der
Grund dafür liegt in dem einfachen Umstand, dass die
meisten Produkte – von Werkstoffen über den Anlagenbau
bis hin zu Gütern des täglichen Bedarfs – weiterhin in Fa-
briken hergestellt werden müssen. Die industrielle Produktion wird sogar noch anwachsen, weil auch die ›Intelligent
Technology‹ für ihre innovativen Erzeugnisse auf Produktionsstätten angewiesen ist.

Industriebau: Wegbereiter der Moderne

Auf die Architektur bezogen heißt dies, dass Rolle und
Bedeutung des Industriebaus keineswegs schwinden werden. Im Gegenteil: Was man ebenso schlicht wie treffend
als ›Zweckbau‹ bezeichnet, wird sich in Zukunft mit neuen
Ansprüchen und Herausforderungen auseinander zu set-
zen haben. Nimmt man die besten Beispiele aus der Ver-
gangenheit, so müsste einem darum nicht bange sein. Ein
Rückblick auf die Geschichte der Architektur seit 1850
zeigt nämlich, dass der ingenieurmäßige Zweckbau die
breite Spur gelegt hat, auf der die Moderne voranschreiten
konnte. In seinem Bereich – und nicht etwa im Wohnungs-
bau oder im Verwaltungsbau – wurden neue statische Sys-
teme erfunden, neue Konstruktionen entwickelt und neue
Werkstoffe erprobt wie Eisen, Glas, Stahl, Beton oder Aluminium. Das Werden einer neuen Architektur drückte sich
zuerst in den Tragwerken und den bis dahin nicht erreich-
ten Spannweiten der großen Hallen für Ausstellungen und
Verkehr aus, in der Gestalt kubischer, undekorierter Baukörper für Industrie und Handel, in der konsequenten Vor-
fertigung von Bauteilen wie beispielsweise beim Londoner
Kristallpalast.[1]
    Die Entwicklung des modernen Industriebaus bedeute-
te zugleich die Emanzipation vom historistischen ›Fabrik-
schloss‹. Anstelle von herrschaftlichen Gebäuden, deren
geschmückte Fassaden die nackte Ausbeutung mensch-
licher Arbeitskraft in Lärm und Gestank verbrämten, for-
derten aufgeklärte Architekten wie Hans Poelzig, Peter
Behrens und Walter Gropius neben zweckmäßigen baulichen Anlagen für die Produktionsvorgänge auch eine
Verbesserung der Arbeitsbedingungen. Vor allem der Ruf
nach Licht, Luft und Sonne hatte nirgendwo sonst mehr
Berechtigung als im Industriebau, der bis ins 20. Jahrhundert hinein durch dunkle Treppenhäuser, enge Flure sowie
durch schlecht belichtete, mit stickiger Luft erfüllte Pro-
duktionsräume geprägt war.[2] Den Forderungen nach einer
humaneren Fabrikarchitektur kamen die neuen Skelett-

Breakthrough to
Industrial Culture
The Märker
Cement Works by
the architects
Ackermann and
Partners

For some years now, a new expression has been doing the rounds in Europe: people talk of the "information society" – and just as often of the progressive dematerialization of all processes of life. The fact is, however, that for the foreseeable future, even highly developed societies will continue to sustain a large part of their production on an industrial basis. The "old economy" will age much less rapidly than futurologists predict. The simple reason for this is that most products – from materials and plant to everyday objects – will still have to be manufactured in factories. Industrial production will, indeed, increase, because even "intelligent technology" is dependent on places of production for its innovative wares.

Industrial building: vanguard of the Modern Movement

In the context of architecture, this means that the role and significance of industrial building will certainly not decline. On the contrary, "functionalist building", as it is simply, yet aptly, known, will be faced with new challenges and demands in the future. Considering the fine examples created in the past, there should be nothing to fear. A glimpse at the history of architecture since 1850 shows that the broad path along which the Modern Movement advanced was forged in large part by functionalist engineering structures. In this field – not in housing or office building – new structural systems were devised, new forms of construction developed and new materials such as iron, glass, steel, concrete and aluminium were tested. The evolution of a new architecture manifested itself initially in the load-bearing structures and hitherto unknown spans of great halls for exhibition and transport purposes; in the plain, unornamented, cubic volumes for trade and industry; and in the extensive prefabrication of elements for buildings such as the Crystal Palace in London.[1]

The development of modern industrial structures also signified their emancipation from the historicist "factory castle" image. In place of grand buildings, the decorated facades of which masked the blatant exploitation of human labour in noisy, foul-smelling conditions, enlightened architects such as Hans Poelzig, Peter Behrens and Walter Gropius advocated not only efficiently functioning buildings to house the production processes, but also an improvement in the working conditions themselves. Above all, the call for light, air and sunshine had no greater validity than in the field of industrial construction, which until well into the 20th century was characterized by dingy staircases, narrow corridors and poorly lit production areas filled with stifling air.[2] The demands for more humane factory architecture were ideally met by the new skeleton-frame structures in steel and reinforced concrete, the open bays of which could accommodate broad glass panels or window strips.

For some companies, progressive forms of building became a synonym for an all-embracing corporate industrial culture. In the years after 1900, this trend was most conspicuous in the structures Peter Behrens designed for the AEG in Berlin; and in the middle of the 20th century, a similar development could be found in the buildings Figini and Pollini created for Olivetti in Ivrea.[3] In the decades following this, however, private commitment to industrial construction declined, as indeed did public interest in developments of this kind. Although industrial building was

the subject of a lively debate throughout Germany down to the period of reconstruction after World War II, since the end of the "economic miracle", it has had an increasingly peripheral status. The serious consequences of this are clearly evident both in cities and the countryside in the form of sprawling industrial and commercial zones, which Egbert Kossak, the long-year municipal chief architect of Hamburg, once described as "urban scrapyards". On the other hand, public awareness of the need for conservation of the industrial-cultural heritage is still underdeveloped. In the Bavarian city of Augsburg, for example, which has a rich industrial tradition, a number of important historical buildings have been demolished in recent years.[4]

A cement works as an industrial landscape

In contrast to other sectors of the economy, the history of construction in the German cement industry has not been adequately researched to date.[5] This is surprising for a number of reasons: firstly, because in the course of the 20th century, concrete was to become the leading construction material; secondly, because in their design, cement works – like conveyor plants in mining, smelting works or refineries – are closely linked to the actual production processes, and this has led to the development of distinctive forms. Thirdly, and most importantly, because of the local availability of the raw materials necessary for their operation, cement works are often situated in the open landscape and not in urban areas. They thus play a role in the progressive "reshaping of the earth's surface", in which, in 1928, the cultural historian Sigfried Giedion recognized a fundamental characteristic of expanding industry: "We push downwards, upwards and across the surface."[6]

In quite a direct sense, many cement works have resulted in the creation of industrial landscapes; i.e. in the conversion of their location to such. This applies specifically to the Märker Cement Works. A splendid panorama unfolds here as one approaches the little Swabian town of Harburg along the federal highway from Donauwörth. The name of the town comes from the palace of the Princes Oettingen-Wallerstein situated high above the valley. Set in a landscape of wooded hills, the striking silhouette of the plant, with its towers, cubes, cylinders and technical apparatus, can be seen from afar. Along the road, it is possible to drive round the entire complex: on the right are lush meadows along the River Wörnitz; to the left is the works with its strict geometric, exposed concrete silos and the slenderly dimensioned steel framework of the kilns – an architectural composition that has been under development since 1958. The skeleton structure of the heat-exchange tower, in contrast, is impressively overlaid with mechanical apparatus.

Forty years ago, the situation was quite different. The family firm, founded in 1889 by August Märker – initially as a "stone and lime works" – had experienced good and bad times economically in the course of its development into an important medium-sized company. (A brief chronicle is included in the appendix to this book.) With the installation of two wet-process rotary kilns and pulverizing plant, cement production was started in 1910 and soon became the most important activity. Furthermore, after World War I, August Märker showed great foresight in purchasing large areas of land around the works – land that contained extensive deposits of raw materials. These acquisitions have guaranteed the existence of the concern down to the present day.

konstruktionen aus Stahl oder Stahlbeton, die sich mit Glas oder Fensterbändern ausfachen ließen, hervorragend entgegen.

Fortschrittliche Bauten wurden bei einigen Unternehmen sogar zum Synonym für ihre umfassende Industriekultur. In den Jahren nach 1900 waren es an erster Stelle die Berliner Gebäude von Peter Behrens für die AEG, in der Mitte des 20. Jahrhunderts die Fabrikanlagen von Figini und Pollini für Olivetti in Ivrea.[3] In den darauf folgenden Jahrzehnten ließ jedoch das private Engagement im Industriebau wie auch das öffentliche Interesse für diese Aufgaben erheblich nach. Gab es in ganz Deutschland bis in die Aufbauphase nach dem Zweiten Weltkrieg hinein eine lebhafte Diskussion über den Industriebau, so wurde in der Bundesrepublik dieses Thema seit dem Ende des ›Wirtschaftswunders‹ zunehmend an den Rand gedrängt. Die gravierenden Folgen sind in Stadt und Land überdeutlich zu sehen: weiträumige Industrie- und Gewerbezonen, die der langjährige Hamburger Oberbaudirektor Egbert Kossak einmal als »städtebauliche Schrottplätze« charakterisiert hat. Auf der anderen Seite ist das Bewusstsein für die Erhaltung des industriekulturellen Erbes noch immer zu wenig entwickelt. So wurden etwa in der traditionsreichen bayerischen Industriestadt Augsburg während der letzten Jahre mehrere bedeutende Baudenkmäler abgerissen.[4]

Ein Zementwerk als Industrielandschaft

Im Unterschied zu anderen Branchen ist die Baugeschichte der deutschen Zementindustrie noch nicht einmal hinreichend erforscht.[5] Dies überrascht aus mehreren Gründen. Erstens, weil der Beton im Laufe des 20. Jahrhunderts zum vorherrschenden Baustoff wurde. Zweitens, weil die Gestalt von Zementwerken – ähnlich Förderanlagen im Bergbau, Hüttenwerken oder Raffinerien – sehr eng an die Produktionsverfahren gekoppelt ist und dadurch besondere Erscheinungsformen hervorgebracht hat. Drittens und vor allem aber, weil Zementwerke auf Grund der für ihren Betrieb notwendigen Rohstoffvorkommen oftmals in der freien Landschaft liegen und nicht in städtischen Regionen. Somit haben sie ihren Anteil an der fortschreitenden »Umgestaltung der Erdoberfläche«, in welcher der Kulturhistoriker Sigfried Giedion bereits 1928 einen Wesenszug der expandierenden Industrie erblickte: »Wir stoßen nach unten, nach oben und in die Fläche vor.«[6]

Zahlreiche Zementwerke haben in einem ganz unmittelbaren Sinne, nämlich aus ihren Standorten heraus, Industrielandschaften geschaffen. Auf das Märker Zementwerk trifft dies in spezifischer Weise zu. Es eröffnet sich ein großartiges Panorama, wenn man sich von Donauwörth her auf der Bundesstraße dem schwäbischen Städtchen Harburg nähert, dessen Name auf das hoch über dem Tal gelegene Schloss der Fürsten Oettingen-Wallerstein zurückgeht: Inmitten bewaldeter Hügel zeichnet sich schon von weitem eine markante Silhouette aus Türmen, Kuben, Zylindern und technischen Anlagen ab. Schließlich kann man auf der Straße das ganze Werk umrunden – zur Rechten die satten Wiesen am Flusslauf der Wörnitz, zur Linken die von 1958 an komponierte Anlage mit den geometrisch strengen Silos aus Sichtbeton und den filigranen Stahlgerüsten der Öfen. Beim Wärmetauscherturm hingegen ist das Skelett von den maschinellen Apparaturen eindrucksvoll überformt.

Vor vierzig Jahren stellte sich die Situation noch ganz anders dar. Das 1889 von August Märker zunächst als ›Stein- und Kalkwerk‹ gegründete Familienunternehmen hatte sich über wirtschaftliche Höhen und Tiefen hinweg zu einem bedeutenden mittelständischen Betrieb entwickelt (eine knappe Chronik findet sich im Anhang dieses Buches), wobei der 1910 mit zwei Nassdrehöfen und Mahlanlagen erneut aufgenommenen Zementproduktion schon bald die entscheidende Rolle zufiel. Hinzu kam, dass August Märker nach dem Ersten Weltkrieg sehr weitsichtig große Rohmaterialgrundstücke in der Umgebung der Werksanlage erworben hatte, welche die Existenz des Unternehmens bis heute sichern konnten.

Mit den Drehrohröfen 1 und 2 begann die Zementherstellung im Märkerwerk. Aufnahme aus dem Jahr 1910

Cement production in the Märker works began with rotary kilns 1 and 2; photo dating from 1910

By the 1950s, the growth of the complex, which included a smaller lime works as well as the extensive cement plant, had led to an unsatisfactory situation: the sequence of operations was based on the old building fabric with its mixture of functions rather than on technical needs. The company, which wished to convert its cement production from an energy-consuming wet process to the more economical dry form of production anyway, was therefore faced with a number of fundamental decisions. Thanks to the mutual efforts of client and architect, a long-term replanning of the works was undertaken, the basic concepts of which have proved their value up to the present day.

Dr Wolfgang Märker, born in 1925 and the grandson of the founder, assumed control of the works in 1960. He found in the Munich architect Kurt Ackermann, who is roughly the same age, a partner who sought an intense dialogue with his clients and who was also specially interested in the continuing development of industrial architecture.[7] Linked by a bond of friendship,[8] these two decisive young men joined forces to shape the future of a cement works that has a long tradition. The relationship between these two strong-willed personalities was not always free of conflict; but after protracted discussions, they always reached a mutually acceptable solution. This also illustrates the "factor of time" that Ackermann regards as so important in the context of industrial building.

The new works evolves

A completely new infrastructure had to be created for the works, which at that time was bounded to the east by the Donauwörth-Nördlingen railway line and dissected until 1970 by federal highway 25. In view of the company goals to extend the range of products and to increase daily cement production from 900 to 3,500 tonnes, the site was completely reorganized. In place of the random layout of the old buildings, a sensible sequence of production facilities was created. A decisive factor in this respect was the

Bauliche Anlagen des Märkerwerks vor 1958

Märker works: built development prior to 1958

disentangling of the functions: for example, the cement dispatch point was transferred from the centre of the works to the end of the production line to the north. Other basic decisions involved the creation of an appropriate traffic circulation system at the centre of the site and the retention of undeveloped areas for later extensions, thus allowing a built response to the economic dynamics of the company.

Since the completion of the "Titan" crushing plant in 1959, the location of which is now occupied by the new circular mixing bed, the work of Ackermann and Partners for the company has extended over a period of 40 years and a number of phases. Important turning points in the technical production of cement were marked by the introduction of the dry process in 1963, and of the roughly 90-metre-long heat-exchange rotary kiln 7 in 1974, which replaced all older plant. In the 1960s, the group of homogenization silos was erected, and later the powerful concrete sculpture of the mixing-bed plant. In the 1970s, these structures were followed by the six clinker silos and the heat-exchange tower – measures that involved crossing the railway line into the "Mollenfeld" area. Parallel to this, a new lime works was created, designed to meet the rising demand on the part of the processing industry. The latest measures are the workshops – taken into operation in the mid-1990s – and the recently completed circular mixing bed.

Architects versus engineers?

People in the cement industry do not generally regard their buildings and production plant as architecture. Their understanding of these structures is determined by specialist engineers whose attitude might pointedly be summarized as follows: "The engineer's thinking and actions are concerned first and foremost with creating a cogent structure, regardless how it looks."[9] That is, indeed, the picture most cement works present. Why, then, is the Märker works in Harburg a rare exception? Why does the plant appear to be so spacious, so well ordered and convincing in its design? One reason for this lies in the client's attitude, his receptiveness to functional and design issues. Dr Wolfgang Märker has thus consciously assumed the cultural responsibilities of an entrepreneur; for, in general, one could say that "without the architectural will of the client, there can be no good architecture".[10]

In view of the technical processes that dominate a complex of this kind, equal importance must be attached to the ability of the architect to convince the engineers of his own concepts, whereby the question of how a productive relationship may be established between architect and engineer is nothing new. As early as 1929, the mining architects Fritz Schupp and Martin Kremmer found clear answers to this question in their book with the curious title "Architekt gegen oder und Ingenieur (Architect versus/and Engineer)".[11] Architects should accept the technical character of an assignment and treat the structure as the supporting framework for the architecture. Engineers, on the other hand, should acknowledge architects as specialists in the fields of urban planning and design and as representatives of the users.

Kurt Ackermann has succeeded in integrating these different requirements to create a model industrial plant – an achievement he shares with his office partner Richard Martin, who has supervised this complex scheme for decades in his role as project architect and construction manager. Their achievements culminate on the one hand in

den eigenwilligen Charaktere war nicht immer konfliktfrei, doch kamen nach langen Gesprächen – hierin liegt der von Ackermann für den Industriebau so wichtig erachtete »Faktor Zeit« – einvernehmliche Lösungen zustande.

Das neue Werk entsteht

Nichts weniger als eine völlig neue Infrastruktur musste für das Werk geschaffen werden, das damals noch nach Osten hin von der Bahnlinie Donauwörth-Nördlingen begrenzt und bis 1970 von der Bundesstraße 25 durchschnitten war. Vor dem Hintergrund der Unternehmensziele, die Produktvielfalt zu erhöhen und außerdem die tägliche Zementproduktion von 900 auf 3.500 Tonnen zu steigern, wurde das Areal neu geordnet. Anstelle der planlos gruppierten Altbauten entstand eine sinnvolle Abfolge der Produktionsstätten. Entscheidend war dabei die Entzerrung der Funktionen, beispielsweise die Verlagerung des Zementversands aus der Betriebsmitte an das Ende der Produktionskette im Nordteil. Weitere Grundsätze galten einer angemessenen verkehrlichen Erschließung im Innenbereich sowie der Freihaltung von Flächen für Erweiterungen, um auf die wirtschaftliche Dynamik der Firma auch baulich reagieren zu können.

Mit dem Vorlauf des 1959 fertig gestellten Titanbrechers, dessen Standort nunmehr das neue Rundmischbett einnimmt, vollzog sich die Arbeit von Ackermann und Partner für das Werk über vierzig Jahre hinweg in mehreren Phasen. Technisch entscheidende Einschnitte in der Zementproduktion bildeten 1963 die Einführung des Trockenverfahrens und 1974 die Inbetriebnahme des rund 90 Meter langen Wärmetauscher-Drehofens 7, der alle Altanlagen ersetzte. In den sechziger Jahren wurde zunächst die Gruppe der Homogenisierungssilos errichtet und anschließend die mächtige Betonskulptur der Mischbettanlage. In den siebziger Jahren – dies bedeutete zugleich den räumlichen Sprung über die Bahnlinie ins ›Mollenfeld‹ – folgten die sechs Klinkersilos sowie der Wärmetauscherturm. Parallel dazu entstand ein neues Kalkwerk, um die steigende Nachfrage der verarbeitenden Industrie befriedigen zu können. Den vorläufigen Abschluss der Neuplanung stellen die Mitte der neunziger Jahre bezogenen Werkstätten sowie das soeben fertig gestellte Rundmischbett dar.

Architekt versus Ingenieur?

»Zementer« betrachten ihre Bauten und Anlagen in der Regel nicht als Architektur. Ihr Verständnis ist geprägt von Fachingenieuren, deren Auffassung sich zugespitzt so charakterisieren lässt: »Das Denken und Machen des Ingenieurs richtet sich zuerst auf eine schlüssige Konstruktion, gleichgültig wie sie aussieht.«[9] So bieten sich denn auch Zementwerke gemeinhin dar. Weshalb aber zählt das Harburger Märkerwerk zu den überaus seltenen Ausnahmen? Warum wirkt diese Anlage so großzügig, so wohl geordnet und gestalterisch überzeugend? Eine Ursache dafür liegt in der Haltung des Bauherrn, in seiner Aufgeschlossenheit gegenüber funktionalen und gestalterischen Fragen. Dr. Wolfgang Märker hat dadurch bewusst auch die kulturelle Verantwortung des Unternehmers übernommen, denn allgemein gilt: »Ohne architektonischen Willen des Bauherrn gibt's keine gute Architektur.«[10]

Gleiches Gewicht hatte die Fähigkeit des Architekten, angesichts der von technischen Vorgängen dominierten Anlage auch die Fachingenieure von seinen Vorstellungen zu überzeugen. Dabei ist die Frage, wie sich ein produkti-

Das Wachstum der Anlage, die neben dem weitläufigen Zementwerk auch ein kleineres Kalkwerk einschloss, hatte in den fünfziger Jahren jedoch zu einem unbefriedigenden Zustand geführt: Der Betriebsablauf richtete sich eher nach der alten, funktional vermischten Bausubstanz als nach den technischen Erfordernissen. Somit stand das Unternehmen, das überdies seine Zementproduktion vom energieaufwendigen Nass- auf das wirtschaftlichere Trockenverfahren umstellen wollte, damals vor grundlegenden Entscheidungen. Dass es dann zu einer langfristigen Werksneuplanung kam, deren Grundsätze sich bis heute bewährt haben, dafür war ein Umstand ausschlaggebend: der gemeinsame Einsatz von Bauherr und Architekt.

Dr. Wolfgang Märker, der als 1925 geborener Enkel des Gründers im Jahr 1960 die Geschäftsleitung übernahm, fand in dem nahezu gleichaltrigen Münchner Architekten Kurt Ackermann einen Partner, dem einerseits an einem intensiven Dialog mit seinen Bauherren lag und der andererseits besonders an der Weiterentwicklung des Industriebaus interessiert war.[7] Zwei junge und entscheidungsfreudige Männer, die außerdem freundschaftlich verbunden waren[8], taten sich zusammen, um die Zukunft des traditionsreichen Werkes zu gestalten. Das Verhältnis der bei-

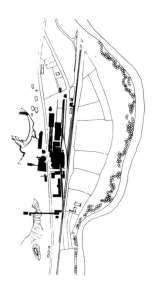

Lagepläne des Märker-
werks 1960 und 1998

Site plans of Märker
works in 1960 and 1998

Anlage der Brandkalk-
aufbereitung, 1978–79

Plant for preparation of
calcined lime, 1978–79

the construction of a series of functional and economical load-bearing structures in concrete and steel, and on the other hand, in the creation of a scheme distinguished throughout by its striking appearance – from the grouping of large, closed volumes to the articulation of the various individual structures. The balance between closed areas and transparency served as a model in this respect; for example, the halls for machinery and materials were enclosed only where protection against the weather or emissions was required. Otherwise, all functions are immediately legible. This "bespoke quality" (Ackermann) to be found in the contrast between closed volumes and multi-layered openness lends the buildings a special, unmistakable plasticity.

The innate sense of continuity in change in the appearance of the Märker works – with modifications resulting from a consistent programme of modernization to meet environmental needs – has its roots in these design principles. The greater quality of the architecture to which this has led has been recognized in the form of numerous top-ranking prizes and a host of laudatory publications. The great breakthrough for the concern was made possible by its investment in qualitative architecture that marks a progression from industrial construction to industrial culture.

Notes

[1] See Kurt Ackermann, "Industriebau und Architektur" in: Kurt Ackermann (ed.), Industriebau, Stuttgart 1994 (4th ed.), p. 66.
[2] Wilhelm Busch provides a summary of German industrial architecture from 1830 in: W. Busch, F. Schupp, M. Kremmer, Bergbauarchitektur 1919–1974, Landeskonservator Rheinland, Arbeitsheft 13, Cologne – no publication date (1980), pp. 9–16.
[3] Further striking achievements in the field of industrial building in the 20th century are documented under the title "Le fabbriche del novecento" in Casabella, 1997/98, vol. 651/52.
[4] Winfried Nerdinger (ed.), Industriearchitektur in Bayerisch-Schwaben 1830–1960, part 1: Augsburg, Architekturmuseum Schwaben, vol. 13, Augsburg 1999.
[5] Axel Föhl, "Bauten der Industrie und Technik", Schriftenreihe des Deutschen Nationalkomitees für Denkmalschutz, vol. 47, Bonn – no publication date (2nd ed. 1996), p. 69.
[6] Sigfried Giedion, Bauen in Frankreich. Eisen, Eisenbeton, Leipzig and Berlin 1928, pp. 7f. – Giedion's plea for modern industrial building caused the cultural philosopher Walter Benjamin to remark that "historically, architecture was the first to outgrow the concepts of art". In: Rolf Tiedemann (ed.), Walter Benjamin, Das Passagen-Werk, vol. 1, Frankfurt am Main 1982, p. 217.
[7] For an introduction to the work of the architect, see Wolfgang Jean Stock, "Building Culture instead of Building Art", in: Ingeborg Flagge (ed.), Ackermann und Partner. Buildings and Projects, Munich and London 1998, pp. 6ff.
[8] See Kurt Ackermann in: Jochen Blumbach (ed.), Wolfgang Märker – in unserer Mitte, private publication, Harburg 1995, pp. 21ff.
[9] Bernhard Tokarz, "Industriebau, eine Entwurfsaufgabe für Ingenieure", in: Kurt Ackermann (ibid, note 1), p. 118.
[10] Benedikt Loderer, "Gute Architektur braucht gute Bauherren", in: Benedikt Loderer, Der Mensch sieht mit den Füßen. 13 Reden zu Architektur und Gestaltung, Glattbrugg 1995, p. 45.
[11] The book is discussed in detail in: Wilhelm Busch (ibid, note 2), pp. 71–84.

Kalkschachtofen III,
fertig gestellt 1979

Vertical lime kiln III,
completed in 1979

Ihre Leistungen kulminieren zum einen in der Konstruktion ebenso funktionaler wie wirtschaftlicher Tragwerke aus Beton und Stahl, zum anderen in der Entwicklung eines prägnanten Erscheinungsbildes, das von der Gruppierung der großen geschlossenen Bauvolumina bis zur Gliederung der differenzierten Baukörper durchgehalten ist. Als Leitbild diente die Balance von Hülle und Transparenz: So wurden die Hallen für Maschinen und Materialien nur verkleidet, wenn es der Witterungs- oder Emissionsschutz verlangte, ansonsten sind die Funktionen unmittelbar abzulesen. Diese »Maßschneiderei« (Ackermann) im Kontrast von Körperlichkeit und mehrschichtiger Offenheit verleiht den Bauwerken eine besondere, unverwechselbare Plastizität.

Die innere Kontinuität im Wandel der baulichen Erscheinung des Märkerwerks – Veränderungen ergaben sich auch durch seine konsequente umweltgerechte Nachrüstung – gründet auf diesen Gestaltungsprinzipien. Der hieraus entstandene Mehrwert an Architektur ist durch mehrere hochrangige Preise und durch viele zustimmende Veröffentlichungen bestätigt worden. Dem Unternehmen selbst hat seine Investition in anspruchsvolle Architektur den großen Durchbruch ermöglicht: vom Industriebau zur Industriekultur.

ves Verhältnis zwischen Architekt und Ingenieur herstellen lässt, keineswegs neu. Schon 1929 hatten die Bergbauarchitekten Fritz Schupp und Martin Kremmer in ihrem Buch mit dem eigentümlichen Titel ›Architekt gegen oder und Ingenieur‹ eindeutige Antworten gegeben.[11] Die Architekten müssten den technischen Charakter der Bauaufgabe und die Konstruktion als Träger der Architektur bejahen, die Ingenieure wiederum die Architekten als Fachleute von Städtebau und Gestaltung sowie als Anwälte der Nutzer anerkennen.

Diese Integration unterschiedlicher Anforderungen in einer beispielgebenden Industrieanlage ist Kurt Ackermann geglückt – zusammen mit seinem Büropartner Richard Martin, der als Projektarchitekt und Bauleiter die komplizierten Aufgaben über Jahrzehnte hinweg betreut hat.

Anmerkungen

[1] Siehe dazu Kurt Ackermann, Industriebau und Architektur, in: ders. (Hrsg.), Industriebau, Stuttgart 41994, S. 66.
[2] Einen Überblick zur deutschen Industriearchitektur seit 1830 gibt Wilhelm Busch in: ders., F. Schupp, M. Kremmer, Bergbauarchitektur 1919–1974, Landeskonservator Rheinland, Arbeitsheft 13, Köln o.J. (1980), S. 9–16.
[3] Weitere markante Leistungen des Industriebaus im 20. Jahrhundert sind unter dem Titel ›Le fabbriche del novecento‹ dokumentiert in: Casabella, 1997/98, Heft 651/52.
[4] Winfried Nerdinger (Hrsg.), Industriearchitektur in Bayerisch-Schwaben 1830–1960, Teil 1: Augsburg, Architekturmuseum Schwaben, Heft 13, Augsburg 1999.
[5] Axel Föhl, Bauten der Industrie und Technik, Schriftenreihe des Deutschen Nationalkomitees für Denkmalschutz, Band 47, Bonn o.J. (21996), S. 69.
[6] Sigfried Giedion, Bauen in Frankreich. Eisen, Eisenbeton. Leipzig und Berlin 1928, S. 7 f. – Giedions Plädoyer für den modernen Industriebau gab übrigens dem Kulturphilosophen Walter Benjamin den Anlass für seine Feststellung, »dass die Architektur am frühesten dem Begriffe der Kunst historisch entwachsen ist«. In: Rolf Tiedemann (Hrsg.), Walter Benjamin, Das Passagen-Werk, Band 1, Frankfurt am Main 1982, S. 217.
[7] Zur Einführung in das Werk des Architekten siehe Wolfgang Jean Stock, Baukultur statt Baukunst, in: Ingeborg Flagge (Hrsg.): Ackermann und Partner. Bauten und Projekte, München und London 1998, S. 6 ff.
[8] Siehe Kurt Ackermann in: Jochen Blumbach (Red.), Wolfgang Märker – in unserer Mitte, Privatdruck, Harburg 1995, S. 21 ff.
[9] Bernhard Tokarz, Industriebau, eine Entwurfsaufgabe für Ingenieure, in: Kurt Ackermann (Anm. 1), S. 118.
[10] Benedikt Loderer, Gute Architektur braucht gute Bauherren, in: ders., Der Mensch sieht mit den Füssen. 13 Reden zu Architektur und Gestaltung, Glattbrugg 1995, S. 45.
[11] Das Buch ist referiert in: Wilhelm Busch (Anm. 2), S. 71–84.

This panoramic view shows how the Märker works was developed in a series of stages to attain its present size: a modern industrial landscape between federal highway 25 and the wooded foothills of the Swabian Jura. Dominating this huge complex is the 65-metre-high heat-exchange tower, which forms the centre of the cement production. In the background on the right is the castle of Harburg, which gave the historic settlement on the River Wörnitz its name.

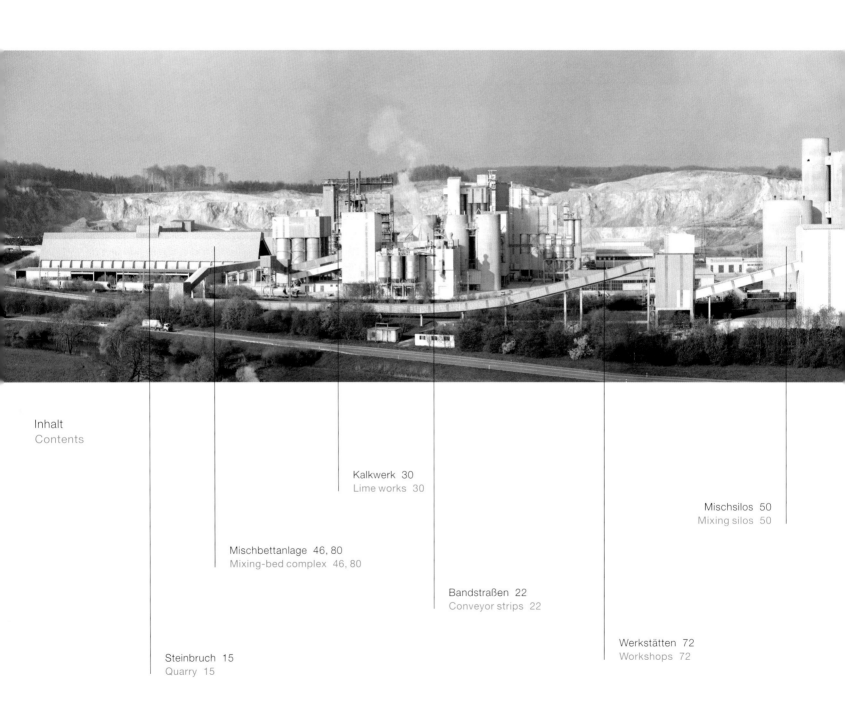

Inhalt
Contents

Dieses Panoramabild zeigt das schrittweise ausgebaute Märker- werk in seiner heutigen Ausdeh- nung. Als moderne Industrieland- schaft liegt es zwischen der Bun- desstraße 25 und den bewaldeten Ausläufern der Schwäbischen Alb. Überragt wird das weitläufige Werk von dem 65 Meter hohen Wärmetauscherturm, dem Mittel- punkt der Zementherstellung. Im Hintergrund rechts ist die Harburg zu sehen, die dem alten Städt- chen an der Wörnitz den Namen gegeben hat.

Rohmühle
und Elektrofilter 56
Raw mill and filter 56

Zementmühle 68
Cement mill 68

Klinkersiloanlage 68
Clinker silos 68

Drehofen 7 64
Rotary kiln 7 64

Harburg

Wärmetauscherturm 58
Heat-exchange tower 58

Leitstand und Labors
Control centre and laboratories

13

Ausgangspunkt der Kalk- und Zementproduktion ist der Abbau der Rohstoffe im Steinbruch. Das Bild zeigt den modernen Steinbruch Bräunlesberg.

Starting point of lime and cement production: excavation of raw material in the quarry. The picture shows the modern Bräunlesberg quarry.

**Das Märkerwerk –
ein Industriebau
als Spiegel
der Produktion**

Der Ursprung des Unternehmens
geht auf eine soziale Tat zurück. In
den achtziger Jahren des 19. Jahrhunderts gründete Karl Märker
zusammen mit seinem Bruder
August und Gleichgesinnten in
Augsburg einen Verein zur Volks-
erziehung. Dessen Ziel war es, die
Not von Großstadtkindern zu lin-
dern. Durch das Entgegenkom-
men des Hauses Oettingen-Wallerstein gelang es dem Verein,
Kindern aus armen Augsburger
Familien während der Sommer-
ferien einen Erholungsaufenthalt
auf der Harburg nördlich von Donauwörth zu ermöglichen. Bei
seinen Besuchen in dem idyllisch
gelegenen Städtchen Harburg
machte der Kaufmann August
Märker auch die Bekanntschaft
eines örtlichen Steinbruchbesit-
zers. Als dieser in finanzielle
Schwierigkeiten geriet, beteiligte
sich August Märker an der Firma
und übernahm sie schließlich.
1889 gründete er dann sein eige-
nes ›Stein- und Kalkwerk‹.

Märker hatte erkannt, dass die
im Harburger Raum zahlreichen
Kalksteinvorkommen gute Aus-
sichten für ein wachsendes Unternehmen boten. Beim fortschrei-

tenden Abbau des Rohstoffs stellte sich allerdings heraus, dass
der Kalkstein zunehmend durch
Ton verunreinigt war. Weshalb am
Rand des flachen und nahezu
kreisrunden Ries-Beckens die
Jurakalke nicht wohl geordnet
lagern, sondern mit anderen Ge-
steinsarten wie beispielsweise Ton
vermischt sind, konnte damals
noch nicht schlüssig erklärt werden. Erst im Jahr 1960 lieferten
zwei amerikanische Geophysiker
den Nachweis, dass der Rieskra-
ter mit einem Durchmesser
von über 20 Kilometern vor rund
15 Millionen Jahren durch den
Einschlag eines riesigen Stein-
meteoriten entstanden war.

Will man den gemischten ›Bo-
denschatz‹ industriell verwerten,
so verursacht er einerseits einen
wirtschaftlichen Nachteil, weil die
Rohstoffe getrennt werden müs-

Der Rohstoff Kalkstein
wird in den Steinbrüchen
traditionell durch Bohren
und Sprengen gewon-
nen.

Limestone – traditionally
extracted from the quar-
ries by means of boring
and blasting

The Märker works –
an industrial
complex as a mirror
of production

The company has its origins in a social act. In the 1880s, Karl Märker, his brother August and other like-minded people in Augsburg founded a society for public education. Its aim was to relieve the plight of children living in big cities. With the help of the House of Oettingen-Wallerstein, the society was able to provide the children of poor Augsburg families with a summer holiday on the Harburg, north of Donauwörth. On one of his visits to the idyllically situated little town of Harburg, the businessman August Märker made the acquaintance of the owner of a local stone quarry. When the latter ran into financial difficulties, August Märker purchased a share in the firm and ultimately took it over completely. In 1889, he then founded his own "stone and lime works".

Märker had recognized that the rich reserves of lime in the Harburg area provided a solid basis for an expanding enterprise. As more and more of the raw material was extracted, though, it became apparent that the lime was increasingly mixed with clay

impurities. Exactly why the Jurassic limestone at the edge of the flat and virtually circular Ries basin did not follow regular beds, but was mixed with other deposits such as clay, was something that could not be plausibly explained at the time. Only in 1960 was it proved by two US geophysicists that the Ries crater – more than 20 kilometres in diameter – had been caused by the impact of a gigantic meteorite roughly 15 million years ago.

One economical drawback to the exploitation of the mixed "mineral resources" on an industrial basis is the fact that the various raw materials have to be segregated before they can be used. On the other hand, there can also

Aufgrund einer weit-
sichtigen Vorratspolitik
erstrecken sich die
Abbauflächen des
Märkerwerks über einen
Kilometer weit nach
Westen in das waldige
Gelände.

The Märker works'
quarrying areas extend
for more than a kilo-
metre into the wooded
landscape to the west of
the plant. They are the
result of far-sighted
policies to secure re-
serves of raw materials
for the future.

Radlader schaffen das
Gestein auf den fahr-
baren Brecher.

Wheeled loaders
transport the stone to
a mobile crushing
machine.

be a distinct advantage in the extraction of a mixture of limestone
and clay. August Märker demonstrated his foresight in finding a
use for the unexpected presence
of the "clay overburden". In 1906,
two years before the large-scale
fire that was to destroy the old
plant, the Märker works started
cement production. The real
boost for the cement works, however, came after World War II,
during the "economic miracle" in
Germany, when there was a con-
stantly rising demand from the
building industry for this material.
   As described in the introduction to this book, it became apparent at the end of the 1950s
that the Märker works would not
be able to guarantee its future in
the long term unless the entire

Der Lageplan zeigt den Verlauf der langen Bandstraße zwischen dem Steinbruch Bräunlesberg und dem heutigen Werksgelände. Rechts unten das neue Rundmischbett.

The site plan shows the route of the long conveyor belt between the Bräunlesberg quarry and the present-day works. On the right at the bottom is the new circular mixing bed.

sen. Auf der anderen Seite bedeutet er aber auch einen Vorteil, weil Kalkstein und Ton gleichzeitig abgebaut werden können. Für den unverhofft aufgetretenen ›Tonabraum‹ fand August Märker eine weitsichtige Verwendung: 1906, zwei Jahre vor dem Großbrand, der dann die alten Anlagen zerstören sollte, nahm das Märkerwerk die Zementherstellung auf. Der wesentliche Schub für das Zementwerk setzte nach dem Zweiten Weltkrieg ein, da während des ›Wirtschaftswunders‹ die Nachfrage der Bauwirtschaft ständig zunahm. Wie in der Einführung zu diesem Buch dargelegt, war am Ende der fünfziger Jahre aber auch deutlich geworden, dass das

plant underwent a complete programme of replanning. An initial step in this direction was taken in 1963 with the introduction of the more economical dry process in the cement works.

One thing has not changed, though: the production still begins in the quarries, where the raw materials, limestone and clay are extracted by means of bulldozing, boring and blasting. The new quarry on Bräunlesberg is the company's most modern extraction site. Excavators and wheeled loaders hoist the broken stone on to heavy lorries or transport it directly to a mobile crush-

ing plant, which reduces the material to pieces roughly 400 mm in size. From here, it is conveyed along a continuous covered strip that snakes its way over a distance of 1.2 km through the wooded landscape. The strip terminates in a structure on the edge of quarry above the works, where the lime is tipped down and loaded on to another conveyor belt for further processing.

Märkerwerk nur durch eine mutige Neuplanung des gesamten Betriebs imstande sein würde, seine Zukunft langfristig zu sichern. Einen ersten Einschnitt stellte 1963 die Einführung des wirtschaftlicheren Trockenverfahrens im Zementwerk dar.

Eines jedoch hat sich nicht geändert: Die Produktion beginnt noch immer in den Steinbrüchen, wo die Rohstoffe Kalkstein und Ton nach wie vor durch Schieben, Bohren und Sprengen gewonnen werden. Der neue Steinbruch am Bräunlesberg ist die modernste Abbaustelle: Bagger und Radlader schaffen das gebrochene Gestein auf Schwerkraftwagen oder

direkt zu einem fahrbaren Brecher, der das Material zunächst auf Größen von bis zu 400 Millimetern zerkleinert. Anschließend wird es von der durchgehend überdachten Bandstraße übernommen, die sich auf einer Länge von 1,2 Kilometern wie ein riesiger Wurm durch das waldige Gelände schlängelt. Dieses Band endet in einem Kopfbau auf der Hangkante des Steinbruchs oberhalb des Werks: Dort wird der Kalkstein nach unten abgeworfen und zur weiteren Verarbeitung auf ein Förderband gegeben.

Der fahrbare Brecher übergibt das zerkleinerte Material auf die überdachte Bandstraße, die sich wie ein riesiger Wurm durch das Gelände schlängelt.

The crushed material is transferred from the mobile crushing plant to the covered conveyor strip, which snakes its way across the site.

Am Ende der Band-
straße wird das Material
nach unten abgeworfen.

At the end of the con-
veyor belt, the material
is tipped over the edge
of the quarry face.

Prior to the replanning, which began in 1958, the works resembled a factory plant that had expanded in random fashion and consisted of a large number of provisional structures. Buildings of all different shapes and sizes were squeezed into the tight space between the main road and the railway line. As a result, the smooth flow of materials necessary for efficient operations was impeded.

The spacious layout that now distinguishes the entire complex is particularly evident in the approach to the works between the production plant and the elevated end of the conveyor belt from the Bräunlesberg quarry, where the

material is tipped. This extensive space is dissected by a series of diagonal lines of impressive length, formed by a number of conveyor belts rising and falling on widely spaced stilts. The area resembles a traffic junction, where the various levels and lines are linked at transfer points.

The raw materials used in the works are processed in a number of stages. The optimization of the lines of conveyance for these materials, therefore, formed a

Oben: Blick auf die mit
Metall gedeckte Band-
straße. Rechts: Abwurf-
stelle oberhalb des
Werks. Unten: Knoten-
punkt der Bandstraßen

Above: view of metal-
roofed conveyor belt.
Right: tip above the
works. Below: conveyor
belt intersection.

Vor der 1958 einsetzenden Neuplanung stellte sich das Werk als
eine unkontrolliert gewachsene
Fabrikanlage mit vielen Proviso-
rien dar. Gebäude von ganz unterschiedlicher Größe und Gestalt
drängten sich auf dem engen
Raum zwischen Bundesstraße
und Bahnlinie. Dadurch wurde
auch der für die Wirtschaftlichkeit
des Unternehmens entscheidende Materialfluss behindert.

Welche Großzügigkeit nun-
mehr die ganze Anlage prägt,
zeigt sich besonders im Vorfeld
des Werks zwischen der oberhalb
gelegenen Abwurfstelle als dem
Endpunkt der Bandstraße aus
dem Steinbruch Bräunlesberg
und den Produktionsstätten. Aufgeständerte Förderbänder von
beeindruckender Länge und mit
möglichst großen Stützenabständen durchziehen in an- oder ab-
steigenden Diagonalen diesen

Förderbänder durchzie-
hen das Vorfeld der Pro-
duktionsstätten, unten
eine Übergabestelle.

The approach area to
the production plant
dissected by conveyor
belts; below: a transfer
station

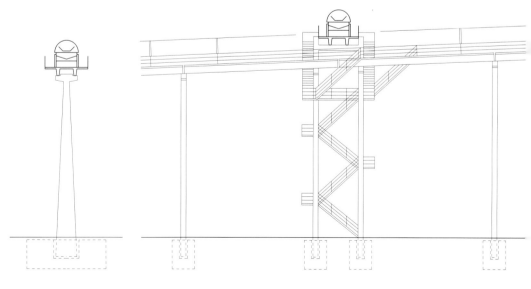

Foto und Schnitt der
turmartigen Siebanlage,
die den Rohstoff klas-
siert.

Photo of and section
through tower-like
screening plant in
which the raw material
is graded

functional starting point for the
replanning programme. In works
of this kind, the conveyor belts
and elevated strips, the transport
spirals and bucket elevators form
the "arteries" of the production
process. Their location and design – reflecting the constraints
imposed by the conveyor system
– determine the position and layout of the built structures such as
the halls, silos and machinery
tracts.

The generous layout of the
area for the conveyor belts pre-
ceding the production plant is
justified by the need to allow suf-
ficient space for the short-term
storage of materials and the
operation of modern large-scale
equipment. The network of
covered conveyor belts is domin-
ated by the tower-like screening
plant, where the raw material
needed for production in the lime
works is gravity sifted.

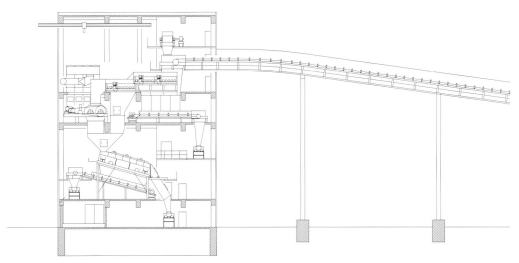

weiten Raum, der wie ein Verkehrskreuz erscheint, weil Übergabestationen zwischen den verschiedenen Ebenen und Richtungen vermitteln.

Die Optimierung der Transportwege für das in mehreren Schritten zu verarbeitende Material bildete nicht umsonst den funktionalen Ausgangspunkt der Neuplanung. Förderbänder und Bandbrücken, Transportschnecken und Becherwerke sind in einer solchen Werksanlage die ›Arterien‹ des Produktionsflusses. Durch ihre fördertechnisch bedingte Positionierung und Ausbildung entscheiden sie auch über den Standort und die Zuordnung von baulichen Anlagen wie Hallen, Silos und Maschinen.

Der den Produktionsstätten vorgelagerte Bereich der Förderbänder ist auch deshalb so großzügig bemessen, damit ausreichende Flächen für die Zwischenlagerung von Material zur Verfügung stehen und der Einsatz von modernen Großgeräten möglich ist. Überragt wird das Netz der überdachten Förderbänder von dem turmartigen Bauwerk der Siebanlage, die unter Ausnutzung der Schwerkraft in erster Linie das Rohmaterial für die Produktion im Kalkwerk sortiert.

Das gesamte Tragwerk der aufgeständerten Förderbänder wurde in Sichtbeton errichtet. Zusammen mit den großen Stützenabständen gibt die silberfarbige Blechdeckung den schlanken Bändern einen eleganten Charakter.

The entire supporting structure of the elevated conveyor belts is in exposed concrete. The wide spacings between the columns, and the silver-coloured sheet-metal roofing lend these slender strips a note of elegance.

Das ausgesiebte ›Unter-
korn‹ wird vor der weite-
ren Verarbeitung im
Kalkwerk zwischen-
gelagert.

The screened fines or
"undersize" is stored in
the lime works before
undergoing further
processing.

Lageplan der Band-
straßen mit dem neuen
Rundmischbett im
Süden des Areals

Plan of conveyor strips
with the new circular
mixing bed to the south

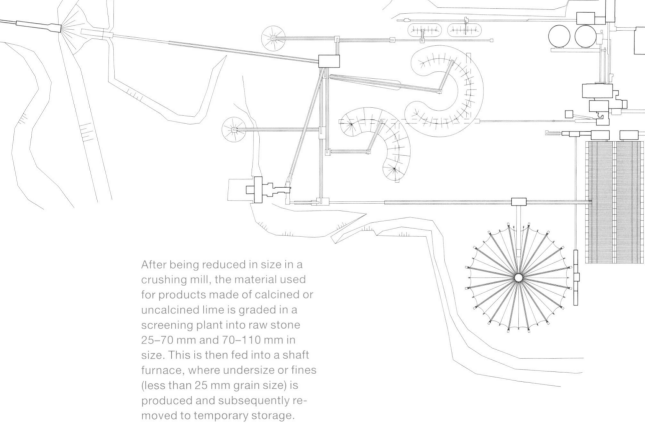

After being reduced in size in a
crushing mill, the material used
for products made of calcined or
uncalcined lime is graded in a
screening plant into raw stone
25–70 mm and 70–110 mm in
size. This is then fed into a shaft
furnace, where undersize or fines
(less than 25 mm grain size) is
produced and subsequently removed to temporary storage.

For cement production, a
crushing mill reduces the coarse
material to a grain size of less
than 60 mm. Still containing
moisture from the quarry, this
substance is loaded on to conveyor belts and transported to a
mixing bed. In addition to the existing linear bed with its striking
form, a circular mixing bed has
been constructed (see site plan).

Für Produkte aus gebranntem oder ungebranntem Kalk klassiert die Siebanlage das zuvor in einem Walzenbrecher nochmals zerkleinerte Gut in drei Gruppen: in Rohkalkstein von 25 bis 70 beziehungsweise 70 bis 110 Millimetern Größe, der dann einem Schachtofen aufgegeben wird, und in feines Material von unter 25 Millimetern, das als ›Unterkorn‹ zunächst zwischengelagert wird.

Für die Zementproduktion zerkleinert ein Walzenbrecher das grobstückige Material auf eine Korngröße von unter 60 Millimetern. Dieses noch grubenfeuchte Gut wird dann auf Förderbändern in ein Mischbett transportiert. Neben dem markanten Längsmischbett wurde inzwischen das Rundmischbett fertig gestellt (siehe Lageplan).

Das große Bild verdeutlicht die weiträumige Anlage des Märkerwerks. Unter dem Förderband zum Längsmischbett hindurch geht der Blick auf die Schachtöfen III und IV des Kalkwerks, die weitgehend transparent gestaltet sind.

The large picture illustrates the spacious layout of the Märker works. The view extends beneath the conveyor belt to the linear mixing bed and vertical lime kilns III and IV, which were designed as largely transparent structures.

Despite its long tradition, the lime works was neglected for decades during the phase in which the cement works was expanding. In 1948, with the founding of the Schwäbische Kalkwerke GmbH, the lime works acquired an independent status within the concern. Nevertheless, the vertical lime kilns I and II remained in service for a long time. For economic reasons, but also because of local circumstances, investments in the lime works were made at a much later date than in the expansion of cement production.

The renewal and extension of the lime works became feasible only when there were clear prospects of re-routing the highway that dissected the site and constricted the activities of the lime production plant in particular. In 1970, the bypass around the site was finally completed.

The first steps in the refurbishment of the lime works date from 1963 and were implemented on the old site. They comprised the erection of new silos and a lime-packing plant. The decisive phase of the extension, however, took place in the second half of the 1970s, following a number of positive developments in the market for lime products. In 1979, the oil and gas-operated cylindrical shaft kiln III was taken into operation, and seven years later the double-shaft kiln IV, powered by coal and gas. Not only was the output increased; the range of products was extended, too, so that parallel to these developments, a new lime dispatch plant was erected.

The Märker works' lime products can be divided into two basic groups. In the manufacture of products from calcined lime, raw limestone of a grain size between 25 and 110 mm is heated in a shaft kiln to temperatures of between 900 and 1,100 °C. The calcined lump lime is initially stored in silos. Part of this is sent out as an aggregate for industrial production elsewhere; the rest undergoes further processing. After crushing and subsequent screening, lime fertilizer is obtained. After grinding, white fine lime is produced; and this, when slaked with water, produces hydrated white lime. These last two products are supplied especially to the building industry; but for some years now, they have also been used in the field of environmental protection.

Undersize is sorted in the central screening plant and used in the manufacture of products from uncalcined lime. After crushing, drying and pulverizing this material, limestone sand is obtained, which is then screened and sifted into various grades and stored in silos. Part of these limestone-sand products are processed in a mixing plant to produce various forms of ready-mixed dry mortar.

Das traditionsreiche Kalkwerk, das jedoch neben dem expandierenden Zementwerk über Jahrzehnte hinweg etwas vernachlässigt worden war, erhielt 1948 durch die Neugründung der ›Schwäbische Kalkwerk GmbH‹ im Unternehmen eine eigenständige Position. Gleichwohl blieben die Kalkschachtöfen I und II noch lange Zeit in Betrieb. Aus konjunkturellen Gründen, aber auch wegen der örtlichen Gegebenheiten wurde in das Kalkwerk später investiert als in den Ausbau der Zementproduktion.

Seine Erneuerung und Erweiterung konnte nämlich erst in Betracht gezogen werden, als sich absehen ließ, dass die das Firmengelände durchquerende und besonders das Kalkwerk einengende Bundesstraße nach außen verlegt werden würde. 1970 war diese Umgehungsstraße schließlich fertig gestellt.

Als erste Maßnahmen zur Sanierung des Kalkwerks wurden noch auf dem alten Areal ab 1963 neue Silobauten sowie die Anlage der Kalkpackerei errichtet. Der entscheidende Ausbau setzte in der zweiten Hälfte der siebziger Jahre ein, nachdem sich der Markt für Kalkprodukte günstig entwickelt hatte. 1979 wurde der Ringschachtofen III für Öl und Gas in Betrieb genommen, sieben Jahre später der Doppelschachtofen IV für Kohle und Gas. Weil nicht nur die Produktion gesteigert, sondern auch die Produktpalette erweitert wurde, entstand parallel dazu eine neue Anlage zur Kalkverladung.

Die Kalkprodukte des Märkerwerks lassen sich im Wesentlichen nach zwei Gruppen unterscheiden. Zur Herstellung von Erzeugnissen aus gebranntem Kalk wird Rohkalkstein in Korngrößen von 25 bis 110 Millimetern in einem Schachtofen auf Temperaturen zwischen 900 und 1100 Grad Celsius erhitzt. Der gebrannte Stückkalk wird zunächst in Silos gelagert. Ein Teil davon geht als Zuschlagstoff für industrielle Produktionen direkt in den Versand,

der andere wird weiter verarbeitet. Durch Zerkleinern und anschließendes Sieben erhält man Düngekalk, durch Mahlen hingegen Weißfeinkalk, der unter Zugabe von Wasser auch zu Weißkalkhydrat gelöscht wird. Diese beiden Produkte gehen vor allem in das Baugewerbe und seit vielen Jahren in den Umweltschutz.

Für Erzeugnisse aus ungebranntem Kalk wird das in der zentralen Siebanlage aussortierte Unterkorn verwendet. Nach Brechen, Trocknen und Mahlen dieses Materials erhält man Kalksteinsand, der dann in einer Sieb- und Sichtanlage in mehrere Fraktionen klassiert und in Silos gelagert wird. Ein Teil der Sande wird in Mischanlagen zu unterschiedlichen Sorten von Werktrockenmörtel verarbeitet.

Vorige Doppelseite: Stückkalksilos aus Sichtbeton, Kalkschachtöfen und Längsmischbett. Die vordere, hoch aufgeständerte Übergabestation im Förderband wird noch mit dem neuen Rundmischbett verbunden. Linke Seite: Zur Vorratshaltung für den Betrieb der Kalkschachtöfen wird ein Teil des Materials im Vorfeld zwischengelagert.

Pages 28–29: lump-lime silos in exposed concrete; vertical lime kilns and linear mixing bed. In the foreground, the transfer station in the line of the conveyor belt is raised on tall stilts. In the meantime, it has been connected to the new circular mixing bed. Opposite page: part of the material is stockpiled on site for operations in the vertical lime kilns.

Der 1979 in Betrieb genommene Kalkschachtofen III nach seiner Fertigstellung, im Hintergrund der nicht mehr bestehende Ofen II

Vertical lime kiln III, taken into operation in 1979, seen here shortly after completion. In the background, kiln II, which no longer exists.

The design strategy on which the Munich architects had based their planning in Harburg from the outset proved its value in the step-by-step extension of the lime works, which continued over a period of more than 20 years.

As Kurt Ackermann stresses in retrospect, each of the construction measures implemented at the works was preceded by extensive investigations: "Initially, we used working models to obtain a visual representation of the layout of the volumes in relation to the flow of materials. The various alternatives developed in the course of these studies were modified over and over again until we achieved a correspondence between the function, the constructional mea-

sures this necessitated, and the formal design. Our design goal was to treat the entire works as a functional machine, in which silos, crushing plant and conveyor systems – together with their constructional skins – were related to each other in terms of location and scale to form a balanced ensemble. The silos, for example, were laid out in such a way that the groups of cylinders have a transparent quality. All structural elements, like prestressing members or bracing ribs, were integrated into the design."

The architectural outcome of this well-considered planning process may be seen as a model for similar industrial building projects, not least because the solutions were achieved in a dialogue with the client and in agreement with the specialist engineers.

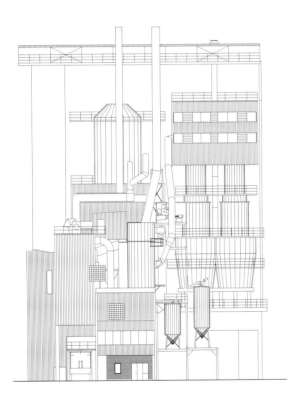
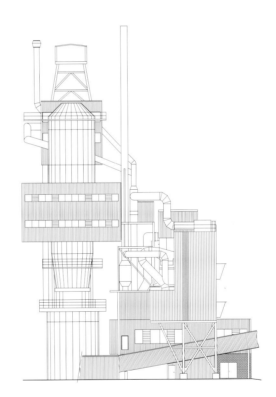

Ostansicht der Kalk-schachtöfen III und IV sowie Südansicht von Ofen III mit den seitlich angebauten Filteranlagen

East elevation of vertical lime kilns III and IV, and south elevation of kiln III, with the filter plant on one side.

The fact that an industrial plant can be more than just a simple combination of mechanical and structural engineering is demonstrated by many aspects of the lime works – from the design of the large-scale volumes to individual construction details. Quite deliberately, the architects have avoided creating container-like halls. Instead, they have taken every opportunity to articulate the many different operations carried out here and to make them legible.

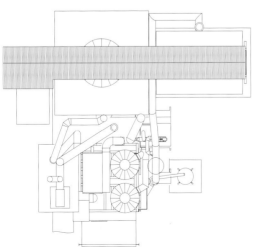

Aufsicht Kalkschacht-
öfen III und IV

Top view of vertical lime
kilns III and IV

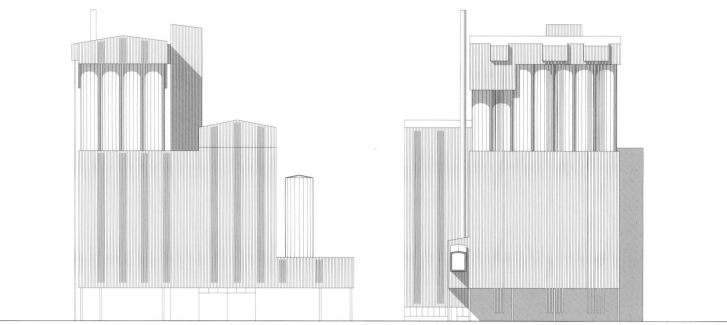

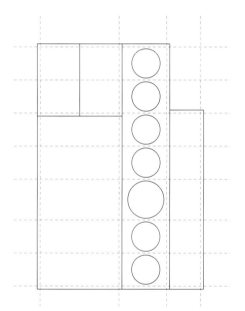

Lineare Anordnung von
Mischanlagen, Kalk-
packerei und Verlade-
silos, darunter eine
Aufsicht

Linear layout of mixing
plant, lime packing area
and loading silos.
Below: diagrammetic
layout

Auch beim schrittweisen, mehr als
zwei Jahrzehnte dauernden Ausbau des Kalkwerks bewährte sich
das Entwurfsverfahren, das die
Münchner Architekten von Anfang
an zur Grundlage ihrer Planungs-
tätigkeit in Harburg gemacht
hatten.

Wie Kurt Ackermann im Rückblick betont, gingen jeder einzelnen Baumaßnahme im Werk aus-
führliche Untersuchungen voraus:
»Zunächst visualisierten wir die
Zuordnung der Baumassen zum
Materialfluss anhand von Arbeits-
modellen. Die bei diesen Überle-
gungen entwickelten Alternativen
wurden vielfach abgeändert, bis
eine Übereinstimmung in der
Funktion, den daraus resultieren-
den konstruktiven Anforderungen
und der Gestalt erreicht war. Un-
ser Entwurfsziel war, das gesamte
Werk als eine funktionale Maschine zu betrachten, in der Silos,
Mühlen und Förderaggregate mit
ihren baulichen Hüllen maßstäblich einander zugeordnet sind. Die
Silogruppen beispielsweise wurden so situiert, dass sie als trans-
parente Zylinder wirken. Alle sta-
tisch konstruktiven Maßnahmen,
wie etwa Vorspannglieder oder
Versteifungsrippen, wurden für
die Gestaltung herangezogen.«

Angesichts seiner architektonischen Ergebnisse ist dieser
sorgfältig gesteuerte Planungs-
prozess ein Vorbild für ähnliche
Aufgaben im Industriebau – nicht
zuletzt auch deshalb, weil die Lösungen im Dialog mit dem Bauherrn und in Abstimmung mit den
Fachingenieuren erreicht wurden.

Aus Gründen des
Schall- und Emissions-
schutzes sind die Anla-
gen teilweise mit Trapez-
blech verkleidet. Trans-
luzente Platten im Profil
der Bleche dienen zur
Belichtung.

The plant is partially
clad in trapezoidal-
section ribbed metal
sheeting to provide
sound insulation and
to prevent emissions.
Translucent sheets with
the same cross-section
as the metal cladding
allow the ingress of
daylight.

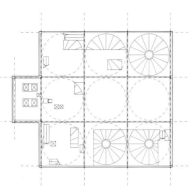

Dieser Horizontalschnitt über alle Ebenen verdeutlicht die modulare Anordnung der Silos.

Horizontal section through the top of the structure, showing the modular layout of the silos

Siloanlage zur Stückkalkaufbereitung: Ansicht der erweiterbaren Halle und Querschnitt durch die Stahlkonstruktion

Silos for processing lump lime: elevation of extendable hall and section through steel structure

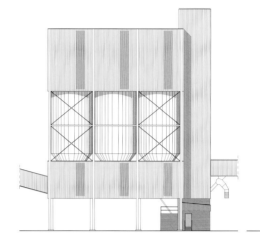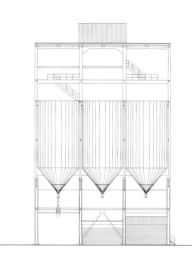

The buildings, for example, which are largely cubic in form, are clad only in clearly defined areas: to protect machines and materials against the effects of the weather, and to protect the surroundings from noise and dust pollution. A lively interplay of open and closed bays led to the creation of a series of structures with individual, memorable facades. In this way, the specific character of the production processes is reflected in the architecture.

Teilschnitt durch die Mischanlagen 4 und 5 des Kalkwerks. Das untere Foto zeigt die konsequente Ausbildung der vertikal betonten Stahltragwerke.

Part section through mixing plants 4 and 5 for the lime works. The photo below shows the systematic design of the steel load-bearing structure with its vertical accentuation.

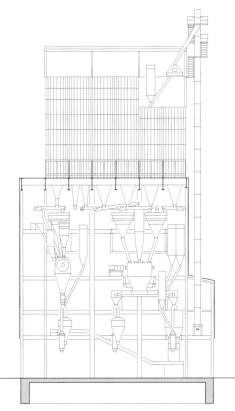

Foto und Ansicht der
Sandanlage mit aufge-
ständerten Stahlsilos.
Auch in diesem Bereich
des Kalkwerks sorgen
offene Erdgeschoss-
zonen für eine groß-
zügige Durchsicht.

Photo and elevation of
raised steel silos for the
storage of limestone-
sand. In this area of the
lime works, too, unen-
closed ground-floor
zones allow extensive
views through the struc-
tures.

Dass eine Fabrik mehr bedeuten
kann als nur die schlichte Verbindung von Maschinenbau mit Trag-
werksplanung, zeigt das Kalkwerk
von der Gestalt der Großformen
bis hin zu den konstruktiven Details. Mit Bedacht haben es die Architekten vermieden, die Hallen
als Container erscheinen zu lassen. Vielmehr haben sie jede der
vielfältigen Chancen genutzt, die
unterschiedlichen Betriebsabläufe
weitgehend sichtbar und damit
ablesbar zu machen.

So wurden die überwiegend
kubischen Baukörper lediglich in
klar definierten Bereichen verkleidet, um Maschinen und Materiali-
en vor Witterungseinflüssen oder
die Umgebung vor Emissionen
wie Lärm und Staub zu schützen.
Durch den spannungsreichen
Wechsel von offenen und ge-

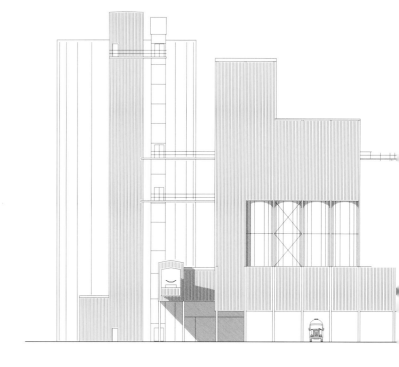

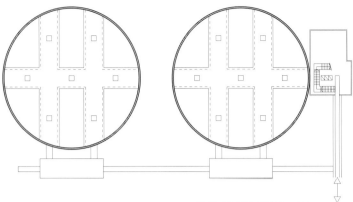

In den beiden Silobauten
aus Sichtbeton wird der
gebrannte Stückkalk
gelagert.

Calcined lump-lime is
stored in the two ex-
posed-concrete silos.

The overall appearance is nevertheless perceived as a visual unity.
Specific building forms, structures and materials were system-
atically assigned to certain functions. For example, large con-
tainers, like the two lump-lime
silos, were executed in exposed
concrete. In contrast, the smaller
silos within the buildings are in
steel. In 1979, the Federation of
German Architects (BDA) in
Bavaria acknowledged the quality
of the lime works with an award:
"The clear legibility of elements,
such as the kilns, the load-bearing and bracing members and the
enclosing surfaces, is the outcome of a successful collaboration between the architects and
the company engineers."

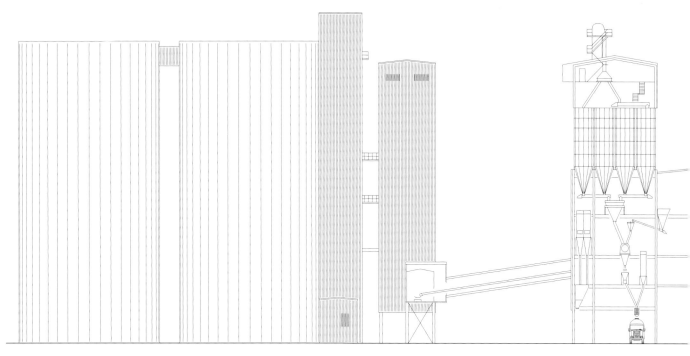

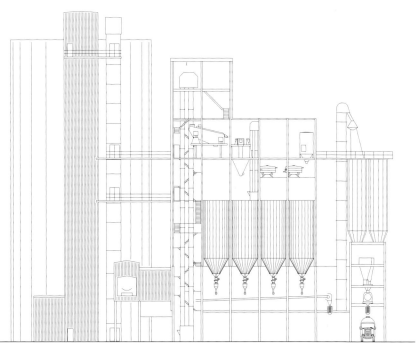

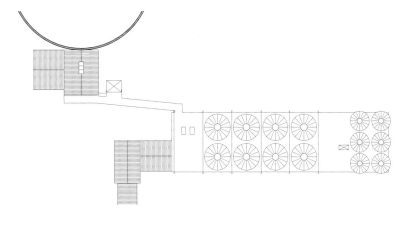

Oben: Stückkalksilos,
Sandanlage und Schnitt
durch die Mischanlagen
4 und 5. Links: Schnitt
sowie Aufsicht von
Sandanlage und Misch-
anlage 3

Above: lump-lime silos,
limestone-sand silos
and section through
mixing plants 4 and 5.
Left and below: section
through and top view
of limestone-sand silos
and mixing plant 3

schlossenen Feldern sind Gebäude mit individuellen, einprägsa-
men Fassaden entstanden: Auf
diese Weise spiegelt sich der je-
weilige Charakter der Produktion
in der Architektur.

Dennoch stellt sich das Erscheinungsbild als eine visuell er-
fahrbare Einheit dar. Bauformen,
Konstruktionen und Materialien
wurden den unterschiedlichen
Aufgaben konsequent zugeordnet. So sind große Behälter wie
die beiden Stückkalksilos in Sichtbeton ausgeführt, die kleineren Silos innerhalb der Gebäude hingegen in Stahl. Im Jahr 1979 erhielt
das Kalkwerk vom Bund Deut-
scher Architekten (BDA) in Bayern
eine Auszeichnung: »Die klare Ab-
lesbarkeit von Elementen wie
Brennbehältern, tragenden und
aussteifenden Teilen sowie umhül-
lenden Flächen ist das Ergebnis
einer erfolgreichen Zusammenarbeit von Architekten und Betriebs-
ingenieuren.«

Die modulare Reihung
der Verladesilos ist in
den beiden rechten
Zeichnungen um eine
Achse erweitert.

In the two drawings on
the right, the modular,
linear layout of the loading silos has been ex-
tended by one bay.

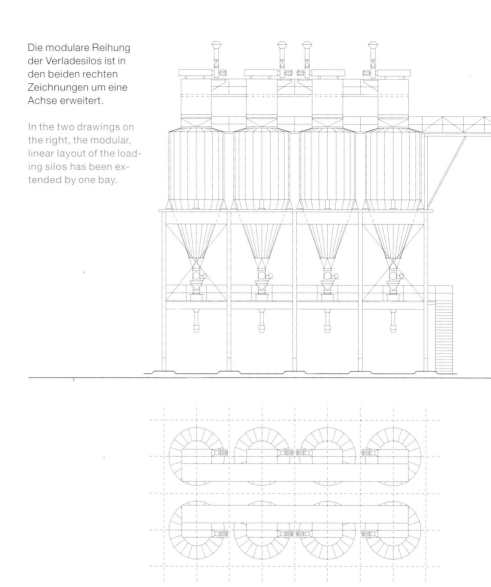

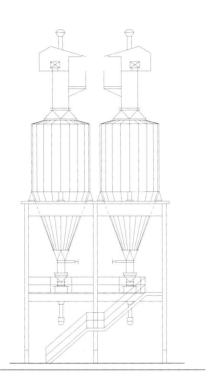

Vorige Doppelseite: Die
sechs unverkleideten
Verladesilos aus Stahl
bilden den Endpunkt
des Produktionsflusses
im Kalkwerk. Linke Sei-
te: Blick von den frei
stehenden Verladesilos
auf die Halle der Sand-
anlage

Pages 42 and 43: the six
unclad steel loading si-
los form the end of the
production line in the
lime works. Opposite
page: view from the
free-standing loading
silos to the hall of the
limestone-sand plant

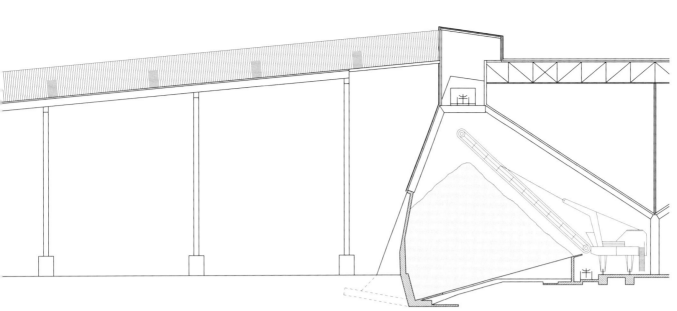

Schnitt durch die westliche Hälfte des Längsmischbetts: Das Profil des Betonskeletts berücksichtigt auch die viertelkreisförmige Bewegung des Kratzers.

Section through the western half of the linear mixing bed: the cross-section of the concrete skeleton-frame structure reflects the quarter-circle movement of the face shovel.

Acclaimed by a long list of publications, the linear mixing bed – taken into operation in 1968 and roofed over in the meantime to provide protection against the weather – has gone into the history of 20th-century industrial building as a masterpiece of functional architecture.

It was originally built to overcome a weakness in the technical processes of the plant. The unchanging composition of materials is a major factor in ensuring constant quality in the production

of cement clinker and the cement into which it is ground. After the conversion to the dry production process at the plant, it was not always possible to maintain this level of quality on an economical basis, using the relatively small homogenization silos, which were completed in 1964 (see next chapter).

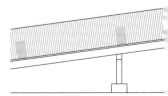

Das ursprünglich offene Skelett des Mischbetts wurde später aus Gründen des Wetterschutzes überdacht. Die durch ihre symmetrische Gestalt markante Anlage gilt als ein Klassiker des Industriebaus.

The open skeleton frame of the mixing bed was later roofed over to provide protection against the weather. The structure, with its bold symmetrical form, is now regarded as a classic of modern industrial construction.

Das 1968 in Betrieb genommene, zwischenzeitlich jedoch aus Gründen des Wetterschutzes überdachte Längsmischbett ist als ein Meisterwerk der funktionalen Architektur durch zahlreiche Veröffentlichungen in die Industriebaugeschichte des 20. Jahrhunderts eingegangen.

Den Anlass für seine Errichtung bildete ein verfahrenstechnisches Defizit. Eine wesentliche Voraussetzung für die gleichmäßige Qualität der Zementklinker und des daraus ermahlenen Zements ist die gleich bleibende Zusammensetzung des Rohmaterials. Nach der Umstellung auf das Trockenverfahren war dieses Qualitätssoll durch die 1964 fertig gestellten, aber verhältnismäßig kleinen Homogenisierungssilos (siehe nächstes Kapitel) nicht immer oder nur unwirtschaftlich zu erreichen.

In der Mischbettanlage wird das zerkleinerte Rohmaterial zu zwei parallelen, etwa 120 Meter langen und 15 Meter hohen Hal-

Übergabestation des neuen Rundmischbetts vor dem Längsmischbett

Transfer station for new circular mixing bed.
In the background: the linear mixing bed

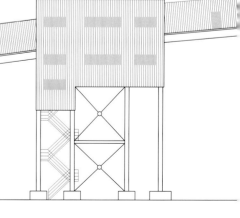

47

Grundriss der ursprünglich
offenen Anlage

Plan of linear mixing bed,
which was originally not
covered.

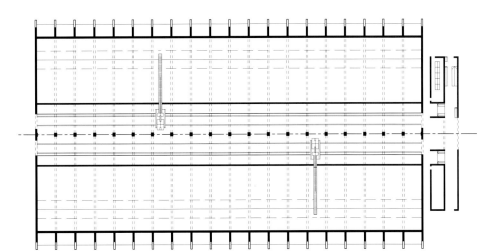

In the mixing-bed tract, the
crushed raw material is heaped
into two parallel mounds roughly
120 metres long and 15 metres
high. At any time, one of these
mounds is in the process of being
built up, while the other is being
depleted through the use of the
material. So-called "face shovels" remove the stockpiled material layer by layer and load it on to
conveyor belts on which it is
taken for further processing. This
method ensures an optimum mixing of the material and evens out
any fluctuations in its composition resulting from the geological
conditions in the quarry.

The striking outline of the linear mixing-bed structures, which
are based on the weekly needs of
the works, is the outcome of the

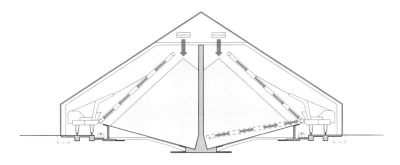

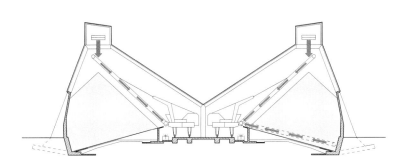

den aufgeschüttet, von denen sich eine im Aufbau und eine im Abbau befindet. Nach dem Aufschütten bauen so genannte Kratzer die Halde schichtweise wieder ab und bringen das Material zur weiteren Verarbeitung auf Förderbänder. Diese Methode führt zu einer optimalen Durchmischung und gleicht so die durch die geologischen Verhältnisse im Steinbruch bedingten Schwankungen aus.

Das einprägsame Profil der auf Wochenbedarf ausgelegten Anlage hat sich aus folgenden funktionalen Faktoren ergeben: Querschnitt der Halden, mittig angeordnete Förderbänder, viertelkreisförmige Bewegung der Kratzer sowie deren notwendiger Freiraum über den Schüttkegeln. Der dominante Baustoff ist Stahlbeton, Rahmen und Stützwandscheiben sind Stahlbetonfertigteile.

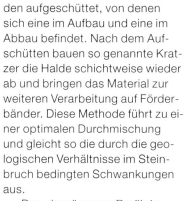

Aus funktionalen und gestalterischen Gründen wurden auch beim Längsmischbett Planungsalternativen untersucht. Die Schemazeichnung rechts unten zeigt den Materialfluss im Mischbett mit den mittig angeordneten Förderbändern.

For functional and design reasons, a number of alternatives were explored during the planning of the linear mixing bed. The diagram (bottom right) shows the flow of materials in the mixing bed, with central conveyor belts.

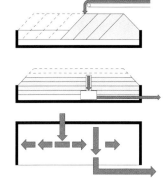

Schnitt durch die 1963/64 errichtete Homogenisierungsanlage mit vorgesehener Erweiterung, links oben das Mischkammersilo

Layout of homogenization plant, erected in 1963–64, showing the planned extension and the mixing silo (top left).

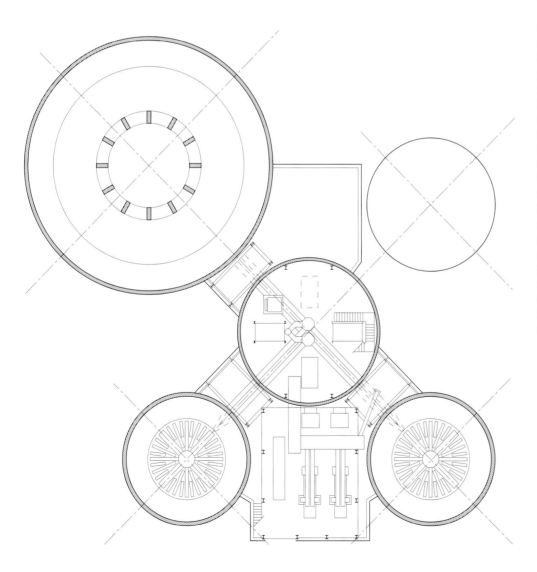

following functional constraints: the cross-section of the piles of material; the central position of the conveyor belts; the quarter-circle movement of the face shovels; and the requisite operating space above the tops of the mounds. The dominant material used for the construction here is reinforced concrete, with frame and retaining wall elements in precast concrete.

As the first stage of construction in the long-term replanning of the complex, the homogenization plant for the cement works was erected in 1963–64. Functionally, the plant is already part of history, since the silos no longer serve to provide a consistent mixture of materials. They are now used as additional storage space for raw meal to compensate, for example, for any shortages or irregularities during operations. But even changes of use of this kind may be seen as an expression of the dynamic development of the concern.

The starting point of the original planning programme was the conversion of cement production to the dry process. In the old wet process, the mixing and homogenization of the pulverized raw material was carried out with the addition of water; but this meant that large amounts of energy were consumed in drying out the substance before the clinker could be fired. In the dry process, the raw meal is mixed with the aid of air. A long series of experiments had shown that, under certain circumstances, the mixture of raw meal and air could be made just as fluid as a suspension of raw meal in water. This complied with the conditions for stable kiln operations and a constant, competitive quality.

Als erster Bauabschnitt im Rahmen der langfristigen Neuplanung des Werks wurde 1963/64 die Homogenisierungsanlage des Zementwerks errichtet. Von ihrer Funktion her ist die Anlage bereits ein historisches Zeugnis, weil die Silobauten nicht mehr der Vergleichmäßigung des Materials dienen, sondern als zusätzliche Lagerkapazität für Rohmehl, um beispielsweise betriebliche Störungen ausgleichen zu können. Auch in solchen Nutzungsänderungen drückt sich die dynamische Entwicklung des Unternehmens aus.

Ausgangspunkt der seinerzeitigen Planung war die Umstellung der Zementproduktion auf das Trockenverfahren. Beim alten Nassverfahren erfolgte die Mischung und Homogenisierung des gemahlenen Rohstoffs unter Zugabe von Wasser, das aber unter hohem Energieaufwand wieder verdampft werden musste, ehe der Klinker gebrannt werden konnte. Beim Trockenverfahren hingegen erfolgt die Vermischung des Rohmehls mit Hilfe von Luft. Eine lange Versuchsreihe hatte ergeben, dass das Rohmehl-Luft-Gemisch unter bestimmten Bedingungen ebenso fließfähig ist wie eine Suspension von Rohmehl in Wasser.

Somit ist die Voraussetzung für einen stabilen Ofenbetrieb und eine gleichmäßige, wettbewerbsfähige Qualität gegeben.

Allerdings bedeutete die Umstellung für das Märkerwerk ein erhebliches Risiko, da zunächst fraglich war, ob sich die neue Methode angesichts der schwierigen Harburger Rohmaterialverhältnisse überhaupt einsetzen ließ. Trotz mancher Bedenken entschloss sich aber die Firma unter Führung von Dr. Wolfgang Märker zur Einführung des Trockenverfahrens, weil es sich durch einen wesentlich niedrigeren Energieverbrauch

Das Erscheinungsbild der schlanken Homogenisierungssilos wird durch die Rippen der Vorspannung geprägt.

The slender appearance of the homogenization silos is distinguished by the shallow ribs containing prestressing tendons.

The conversion nevertheless involved a considerable risk for the Märker works: initially, it was uncertain whether the new method could be implemented, in view of the problematic nature of the raw materials in Harburg. Despite certain reservations, the company, with Dr Wolfgang Märker at its head, decided in favour of the dry process, since it promised a considerable reduction of energy consumption. Ultimately, this proved to be the right decision, because it ensured the survival of the company in times of rising energy prices.

In this project, as in other major sections of the construction programme, the planning process was strongly influenced by the complex technical functions involved and by the structural requirements arising from these. The mechanical engineering firm proposed a linear arrangement of the silos for the homogenization plant, with vertical lifting facilities, a staircase tower and a lift located in the spaces between the cylinders.

The architects, Ackermann & Partners, put forward alternative proposals, and these were ultimately implemented, since they offered a convincing functional and design solution. The radial layout of the silos around a central, cylindrical, vertical distribution tower resulted in transport lines of equal length. The proportions and the requisite slenderness of this extendible group of silos were the product of the ratio of diameter to height.

Aufnahme der Homogenisierungsanlage nach 1970. Rechts unten: Schemazeichnung der Funktionen und Schnitt

View of homogenization plant after 1970. Bottom right: functional diagram and section through plant

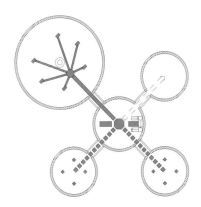

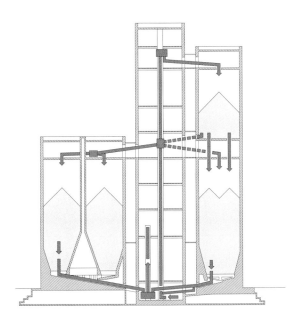

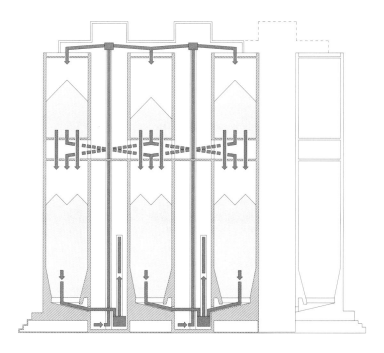

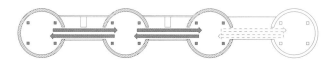

Abgelehnter Planungs-
vorschlag der Maschi-
nenbaufirma

Planning proposals
made by mechanical
engineering company;
subsequently rejected.

auszeichnet. Die Entscheidung
erwies sich als richtig, weil sie
dem Betrieb in Zeiten der Ener-
gieverteuerung das Überleben
gesichert hat.

Wie bei anderen wichtigen
Baugruppen im Werk wurde auch
bei diesem Vorhaben der Pla-
nungsprozess durch die komplizierten technischen Funktionen
und die statisch-konstruktiven
Anforderungen beeinflusst. Die
Maschinenbaufirma hatte für die
Homogenisierungsanlage eine lineare Anordnung der Silos vorge-
schlagen. In den Zwischenräumen
der Zylinderformen waren die
Vertikalförderungsanlagen, der
Treppenturm sowie der Aufzug
angeordnet.

Diesem Vorschlag setzten die
Architekten Ackermann und
Partner eine Alternative entgegen,
die dann auch ausgeführt wurde,
weil sie funktional und gestalterisch überzeugte. Die sternförmi-
ge Gruppierung der Silos um
einen runden Förderturm als zen-
tralem vertikalen Verteiler führte
beim Transport zu gleich langen
Wegen. Die Proportion und der
gewünschte Schlankheitsgrad der
erweiterbaren Silogruppe ergaben sich aus dem Verhältnis von
Durchmesser und Höhe.

Nach vielen Modelluntersuchun-
gen konnte eine wirtschaftliche
und zugleich maßstäblich befriedi-
gende Lösung erreicht werden.
Ein Beispiel für die gestalterische
Optimierung ist die Kopfausbil-
dung der Silos. Früher wurde das
Verteilerhaus für Rinnen und Elektrofilter auf die Zylinderform ge-
setzt. Hier hingegen haben die Architekten in Zusammenarbeit mit
den Ingenieuren die Außenschale
hochgezogen und abgedeckt,
sodass alle Maschinenteile in die
Siloform integriert sind.

Hohe statische Anforderungen
wurden besonders an die 55 Meter hohen, doppelstöckigen Homogenisierungssilos gestellt, die
durch Druck- und Wärmeentwick-
lung stark beansprucht werden.
Die Silowand wurde daher als
Spannbetonschale mit außenlie-
genden Rippen als Widerlager für
die Spannglieder ausgebildet. Die
Rippen sind zugleich ein gestalte-
risches Element, das die Schlank-
heit der zylindrischen Baukörper
unterstützt.

After several exploratory investigations using models, an economical solution was found that was also satisfying in scale. As an example of the process of design optimization carried out here, one might cite the heads of the silos. In traditional forms of construction, it was common to set a distribution structure, containing channels and electric filters, on top of the cylindrical form. In the Märker works, the architects, in collaboration with the engineers, extended the outer skin upwards and closed it off at the top so that all equipment is accommodated within the form of the silo itself.

The 55-metre-high two-storey homogenization silos in particular are subject to heavy structural loading through the generation of pressure and heat. The silo walls, therefore, were designed as pre-stressed concrete shells, with shallow external ribs forming a kind of buttressing in which the stressing tendons are housed. The ribs are also a design element that accentuates the slender appearance of the cylinders.

The external walls of the central lifting tower were executed in reinforced concrete with sliding shuttering. The 61-metre-high tower houses a lift, a staircase and bucket elevators for charging the silos. In the tower, the various levels or stages are constructed of steel sections; in the silos, they consist of precast concrete elements.

Alle Silos der Homogenisierungsanlage werden nunmehr als zusätzliche Lagerkapazität für Rohmehl genutzt. Das Bild zeigt Restmaterial am Boden des Mischkammersilos.

All silos forming part of the homogenization plant are now used as additional storage space for raw meal. The picture shows residual material on the floor of the mixing silo.

Die hohle Mittelsäule
entlüftet die Mischkam-
mer und nimmt die Verti-
kallasten der Silodecke
auf.

The hollow central cylin-
der bears the vertical
loads of the silo roof and
also serves to ventilate
the mixing chambers.

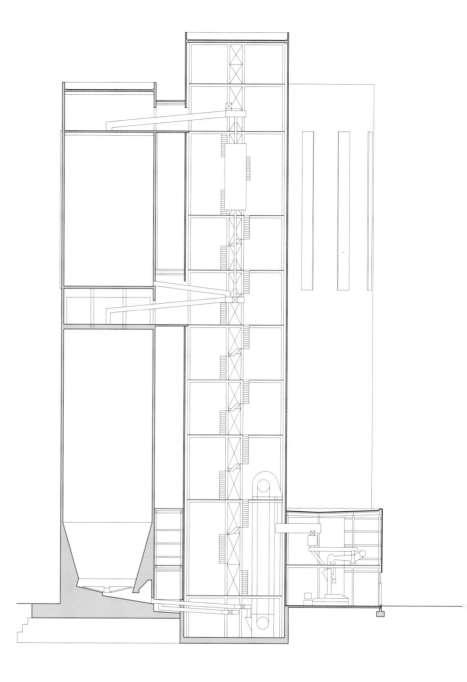

Fotos: Details des ent-
leerten Mischkammer-
silos. Schnitt: zentraler
Förderturm und doppel-
stöckiges Homogenisie-
rungssilo

Photos: details of empty
mixing silo. Section
through central lifting
tower and two-level
homogenization silo.

Auch die Außenwand des zentralen Förderturms wurde in Stahlbeton mit einer Gleitschalung hergestellt. Der 61 Meter hohe Turm
enthält einen Aufzug, die Treppe
sowie die Becherwerke zur Be-
schickung der Silos. Im Turm be-
stehen die Bühnen aus Stahlprofi-
len, in den Silos aus Stahlbeton-
fertigteilen.

Nach dem Firmenentwurf hät-
ten drei nebeneinander angeordnete und durch Zwischenbauten
verbundene Silos wie eine riesige
Wand auf dem Gelände gewirkt.
Das Sternsystem hingegen ergab
eine sachlich-elegante Gruppierung von hoher Durchsichtigkeit.

Diese Anlage bildete den Auftakt
für das neue und charakteristi-
sche Erscheinungsbild des Märkerwerks. 1971 wurde es mit dem
renommierten Architekturpreis
des BDA Bayern ausgezeichnet:
»Das Zementwerk ist ein Industriebau, der in seiner Ausformung
über einen reinen Zweckbau
hinausgeht und damit Rücksicht
auf seine Umwelt nimmt. Dabei
ist die Einheit von Aufgabe, Funktion, Material und Form hervor-
zuheben.«

Ostansicht von Roh-
mühle 5 und Elektrofilter.
Rechte Seite: Blick in
den hohen Innenraum
der Rohmühle

View from east to raw
mill 5 and electrical
filter. Opposite page:
the tall internal space
of the raw mill

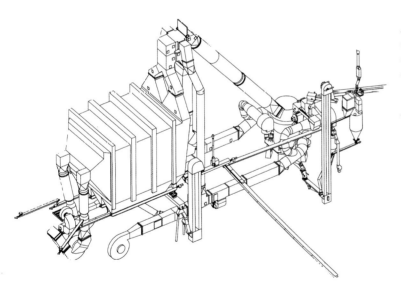

Der aufgeständerte
Elektrofilter zwischen
dem Mühlengebäude
und dem Wärmetau-
scherturm dient zur Ent-
staubung der Anlage.

The elevated electrical
filter between the raw
mill and the heat-ex-
change tower serves to
remove dust from the
plant.

Auch bei der Zementherstellung
gibt es die entscheidende Schnitt-
stelle: den Wechsel von der me-
chanischen zur thermischen Bear-
beitung des Rohstoffs. Walzenbrecher und Mischbett dienen als
Vorstufen, um ihn zu zerkleinern
und zu homogenisieren. Aus dem
Mischbett gelangt das derart vor-
behandelte Rohmaterial über Do-
siereinrichtungen in die Rohmühle. Dort wird es mehlfein gemahlen
und von den etwa 300 Grad Celsius heißen Abgasen des Drehrohr-
ofens getrocknet. Anschließend
wird das Rohmehl in den Silos der
früheren Homogenisierungsanlage zwischengelagert.

Die Rohmühlenanlage ist ein
Stahlskelettbau, der im Erdge-
schoss mit Kalksandsteinen aus-
gefacht und in den Obergeschos-
sen mit verzinktem Trapezblech
verkleidet wurde. Die Stahlkonstruktion wurde gewählt, um den
Maschinen eine Hülle zu geben,
die notwendigen Änderungen
leicht angepasst werden kann.
In der Zementindustrie sind Mahlanlagen einem sehr großen Ver-
schleiß ausgesetzt, außerdem
schreitet die technische Entwicklung der Maschinen stetig voran.
Derzeit ist die Rohmühle 5 in
Betrieb.

Zur Entstaubung der Anlage dient
ein Elektrofilter, der zwischen dem
Mühlengebäude und dem Wärmetauscherturm frei auf einer Stahl-
unterkonstruktion steht, sodass
die Abfolge der Bauten nicht als
geschlossener Riegel wirkt. Der
Filter erfüllt zwei Funktionen, eine
wirtschaftliche und eine ökologi-
sche: Einerseits filtert er aus dem
Strom der Heißluft das Rohmehl
heraus, andererseits reinigt er die
Ofenabgase.

Dieser Filter ist nur eine von
über 150 Entstaubungsanlagen,
die auf dem Werksgelände im
Rahmen der Kalk- und Zementproduktion arbeiten. Durch den
Einsatz von umweltschonenden
Verfahren, wofür bis zu 25 Prozent
der Neuinvestitionen aufgewendet
wurden, konnte vor allem der
Staubauswurf des Zementwerks
drastisch reduziert werden. Heute
emittiert das Werk weniger als ein
Tausendstel der Staubmenge von
vor dreißig Jahren. Dies erhöhte
nicht nur die Arbeitsplatzqualität
im Werk selbst, sondern auch die
Lebensqualität in der Umgebung,
die früher von einer weißen Staub-
schicht bedeckt war.

The three silos foreseen in the company's original plans were laid out next to each other and linked by intermediate structures, so that they would have appeared as a huge closed wall. The choice of a radial arrangement, in contrast, resulted in a functional yet elegant ensemble with a high degree of transparency. This plant marked the first step towards creating a new, distinctive image for the Märker works. In 1971, it was awarded the coveted Architecture Prize of the BDA in Bavaria: "The cement works is an industrial building that, in its design, is more than just a functional structure; it also shows consideration for the environment. In this context, special mention should be made of the unity that was achieved between the brief, the function, the materials and the form."

A crucial interface exists in the production of cement as well: at the transition from mechanical to thermal processing of the raw material. In the preliminary stages, the material is reduced in size in a crushing mill and homogenized in the mixing bed. From here, the pretreated raw material is batch-fed into a raw mill, where it is ground to a powdery consistency and dried by the exhaust gases from the rotary kiln at a temperature of 300 °C. Finally,

the raw meal is stored temporarily in the silos of the former homogenization plant.

The raw mill is a steel skeleton-frame structure, with sand-lime-brick infill panels at ground floor level and with galvanized trapezoidal-ribbed metal sheeting to the upper floor levels. A steel structure was chosen so as to enclose the machinery in a protective housing that can be easily adapted to changing circumstances. The milling plant in the cement industry is subject not only to great wear and tear, but to a constant process of technical development. At the moment, raw mill number five is in operation.

An electrical filter is used to remove dust. The filter is situated on an independent steel structure between the raw mill and the heat-exchange tower, so that the sequence of buildings does not appear as a continuous, closed tract. The filter serves an economical and an ecological function: on the one hand, it extracts raw meal from the stream of hot air; at the same time, it purifies the exhaust gases from the kilns.

The filter is only one of more than 150 dust-collecting devices operating within the lime and cement production plant. The use of

Der hohe Energiebedarf zum Betrieb des Zementofens wird zu einem Teil durch die Verbrennung von Altreifen bestritten.

The great energy needs for operating the cement kiln are met in part by burning old tyres.

Die für den Umwelt- und Landschaftsschutz erfolgreichen Maßnahmen des Unternehmens sind schon sehr früh offiziell gewürdigt worden: Im Jahr 1979 erhielt der damalige Betriebsleiter Heinz Radewald als einer der ersten Träger die neu gestiftete bayerische Umweltmedaille.

Die Selbstverpflichtung zu einem ökologischen Verhalten zeigt sich im Märkerwerk auch daran, dass der hohe Energiebedarf zum Betrieb des Zementofens zu erheblichen Teilen aus der thermischen Verwertung von ›Abfällen‹ bestritten wird. Als unkonventionelle Brennstoffe werden vor allem Altreifen und Altöle eingesetzt. Für eine günstige Umweltbilanz spricht außerdem, dass man dem Rohmaterial kalkhaltige Rückstände aus Trinkwasseraufbereitungs-

anlagen zusetzt und beim Mahlen des Zements Rauchgasgipse unschädlich entsorgt.

Aber auch die Energiegewinnung durch Recycling hat ihre Grenzen. Für den Einsatz alternativer Brennstoffe im Zementwerk gelten vier wesentliche Bedingungen. Erstens darf sich die Emissionssituation im Werk und seiner Umgebung nicht verschlechtern. Zum Zweiten sind Schäden für die Mitarbeiter beim Umgang mit solchen Stoffen auszuschließen. Drittens darf die Produktqualität nicht leiden und schließlich muss die Produktion auch weiterhin wirtschaftlich sein.

Oben eine Aufnahme
des Wärmetauscher-
turms aus den siebziger
Jahren, auf der rechten
Seite die heutige Anlage

Above: view of the heat-
exchange tower in the
1970s. Opposite page:
the plant today

environmentally-friendly processes of this kind, which account for
up to 25 per cent of the new investment, has resulted in a dras-
tic reduction in the level of dust
emissions from the cement
works. The amount emitted today
is less than a thousandth of that
emitted 30 years ago. This has
not only improved the working
environment within the plant; it
has also enhanced the quality
of life in the surrounding areas,
which were formerly covered with
a layer of white dust.

The company's successful
implementation of measures for
environmental and landscape
protection gained official recog-
nition at a very early stage. In
1979, Heinz Radewald, the works
manager at that time, was one of
the first recipients of the newly
instituted Bavarian medal for the
environment.

This voluntary acceptance of
an obligation for ecologically-

friendly behaviour on the part of
the Märker works can also be
seen in the fact that the high energy requirements for operating
the cement kiln are met to a large
extent from the thermal exploitation of "waste products". Among
the unconventional substances
used as fuel are old tyres and
waste oil. Other aspects of the
positive environmental life cycle
assessment of the works include
the use of calcareous residue
from water purification plants,
which is added to the raw material; and the removal of gypsum
substances from flue gases during the process of grinding the
cement.

There is a limit, however, to
the amount of energy that can be
generated or conserved by
means of recycling. Four basic

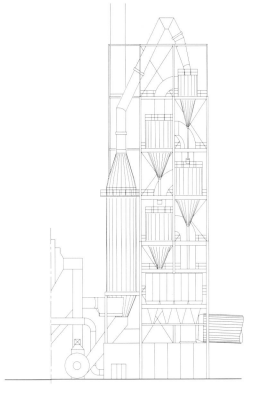

Der Turm des vierstufigen Zyklon-wärmetauschers ist der höchste Bauteil der Drehofenanlage und überragt zugleich das ganze Werk. Die Funktion des Wärme-tauschers besteht in der thermi-schen Verwertung der Ofenabga-se. Über ein Becherwerk wird das Rohmehl zur obersten Zyklonstufe transportiert. Es durchwandert dann die einzelnen Stufen und wird dabei durch den Gegenstrom der Abgase auf über 800 Grad Celsius erhitzt, ehe es dem Dreh-rohr des Ofens zuläuft.

Wegen seiner großen Masse und seiner Höhe von 65 Metern war der Wärmetauscherturm nur schwer in die Umgebung einzufü-gen. Auch bei dieser kompliziert aufgebauten Maschinenanlage führte die Bildung von Alternativen zum Ziel. Nach einem Vergleich der jeweiligen Vor- und Nachteile hinsichtlich Nutzung, Wirtschaft-lichkeit, Konstruktion und ästhe-tischer Wirkung schieden drei unterschiedliche Lösungen in Stahlbeton beziehungsweise Mischbauweise aus. Errichtet wurde eine Stahlkonstruktion, die vom Gedanken her von den ma-schinellen inneren Vorgängen ab-geleitet ist. Neben funktionalen Vorzügen rechtfertigte auch ein idealer Ablauf der Montage diese Lösung. Die unverkleidete Stahl-konstruktion mit minimierten Stüt-zenquerschnitten war darüber hinaus nicht nur flexibel für Verän-derungen, sondern ergab auch eine größtmögliche Transparenz in der Gestaltung.

conditions have been established for the use of alternative fuels in the cement works. First, they should not worsen the emission level within the works and in the surrounding areas. Second, no harmful effects may accrue to staff handling such fuels. Third, there should be no reduction in the quality of the products; and finally, production has to remain profitable.

The tower of the four-stage cyclone heat-exchange plant is the tallest element of the rotary kiln tract and rises above the entire works. The function of the heat-exchange unit is the extraction and exploitation of heat from the kiln exhaust gases. Raw meal is transported to the upper cyclone level by bucket elevators and then passes through the individual stages of the structure. In the process, it is heated to more than 800 °C by exhaust gases flowing in the opposite direction, before it enters the cylinder of the rotary kiln.

In view of its great volume and a height 65 metres, it was not easy to integrate the heat-exchange tower into the surroundings. Here again, the development of a number of alternatives for the complex construction of the machine plant finally led to a

Die Zeichnungen zeigen die Alternativen bei der Planung des Wärmetauscherturms.

Drawings of various planning alternatives for the heat-exchange tower

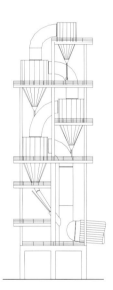
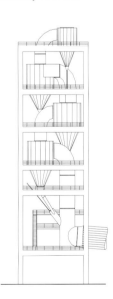
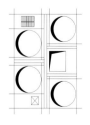

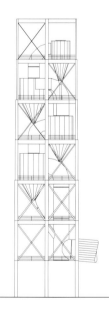

Links ein schematisches
Modell des vierstufigen
Zyklonwärmetauschers,
unten eine Aufnahme
aus den siebziger Jahren

Left: schematic model
of four-stage cyclone
heat-exchange plant
Below: view of the plant
in the 1970s

solution. After an assessment of the pros and cons in terms of function, profitability, construction and aesthetic effect, three alternative solutions in reinforced concrete or mixed forms of construction were dropped. The steel structure that was finally erected is derived conceptually from the mechanical processes taking place internally. As well as the functional advantages it offered, this solution facilitated an ideal assembly sequence. The unclad steel structure with minimized column cross-sections was not only flexible and capable of modification; it also permitted a high degree of transparency in the design.

The history of the cement kilns, with their ever greater dimensions, is in itself a document of the economic development of the Märker works as a whole. In principle, the technology has not changed. The soundness of the

planning and construction of the plant is confirmed by the fact that the first three kilns were in operation for several decades: kilns 1 and 2, indeed, from 1910 to 1966. The introduction of rotary kiln 4 in 1955 marked the first major extension of capacity. With an output of 500 tonnes a day, it was at that time the largest kiln in South Germany. Five years later, it was followed by kiln 5, which had the same dimensions. Then, in 1966, kiln 6, with a capacity of 1,200 tonnes a day, was taken into operation.

The turning point in the extension and conversion of the cement works, however, was marked by kiln 7, which came into service in 1973. A long rotary kiln with a four-stage heat-exchange installation and an output of 3,000 tonnes a day, it replaced all older plants. Since then, this kiln has been the centrepiece of the cement production. All other equipment in this section of the works, from the raw mill to the clinker silos, are organized about it along a linear axis.

The raw meal, heated to more than 800 °C in the heat-exchange plant, passes from cyclone stage 4 to the rotary cylinder of the kiln,

Die Zeichnung gibt den Planungsstand der Zementofenanlage vor 1973 wieder. Zentrum der Anlage ist der 65 Meter hohe Wärmetauscherturm mit den beiden Luftkanälen.

The drawing shows the planning for the cement kiln plant before 1973. At the centre is the 65-metre-high heat-exchange tower with the two air ducts.

Dieses geplante Mischkammersilo wurde wegen technischer Fortschritte nicht ausgeführt.

The planned mixing silo was overtaken by technical developments and was never built.

Rohmühle 4 und Elektrofilter waren bis 1992 in Betrieb.

Raw mill 4 and the electrical filter were in operation until 1992.

Die wirtschaftliche Entwicklung des Märkerwerks lässt sich besonders gut an der Geschichte der Zementöfen ablesen, die immer größere Dimensionen annahmen. Die Technik änderte sich dabei im Prinzip nicht. Für die Solidität von Planung und Konstruktion der Anlagen spricht, dass die ersten drei Öfen viele Jahrzehnte in Betrieb waren, Ofen 1 und 2 sogar von 1910 bis 1966. Eine erste grundlegende Erweiterung der Kapazitäten bedeutete dann 1955 der Drehofen 4, der mit einer Leistung von 500 Tonnen am Tag der damals größte Ofen in Süddeutschland war. Fünf Jahre später folgte der Ofen 5 mit gleicher Dimension, 1966 schließlich der Ofen 6 mit einer Leistung von 1.200 Tonnen/Tag.

Die entscheidende Zäsur beim Ausbau des Zementwerks stellte jedoch der Ofen 7 dar, der 1973 in Betrieb genommen wurde. Als langer Drehofen mit vierstufigem Wärmetauscher ersetzte er bei einer Leistung von 3.000 Tonnen/Tag alle Altanlagen. Seither bildet dieser Ofen das Herzstück

der Zementproduktion. Alle anderen Einrichtungen in diesem Abschnitt, von der Rohmühle bis hin zu den Klinkersilos, sind ihm auf einer linearen Achse zugeschaltet.

Das im Wärmetauscher auf über 800 Grad Celsius erhitzte Rohmehl gelangt von der Zyklonstufe 4 in das Drehrohr des Ofens, wo es bei etwa 1.450 Grad Celsius bis zum Beginn des Schmelzens gebrannt wird. Durch chemische und mineralogische Umwandlung beim ›Sintern‹ entsteht der schwarzgraue, grobkörnige Zementklinker. Er verlässt die Brennzone im 89 Meter langen Drehrohr und fällt in einen Planetenkühler. In den zehn Kühlrohren erfolgt eine Abkühlung auf etwa 130 Grad Celsius.

Als Brennstoff zur Erzeugung der hohen Temperaturen werden Kohle, Öl, Erdgas, Recyclingöl und Altreifen eingesetzt. Die Flexibilität bei der Befeuerung drückt sich in den unterschiedlichen Zubauten am Wärmetauscherturm aus, die dessen ursprüngliches Erscheinungsbild erheblich verändert haben. Nach dem Abkühlen wird der Zementklinker in sechs runden Silos mit einer Gesamtkapazität von 110.000 Tonnen zwischengelagert.

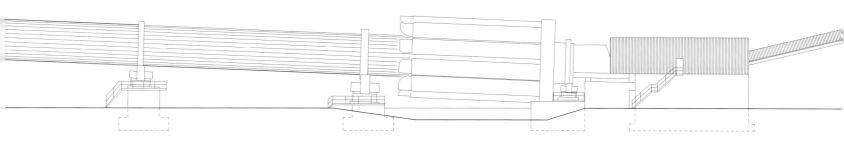

Im 89 Meter langen Rohr des Drehofens 7 entsteht der grobkörnige Zementklinker.

Coarse cement clinker is produced in the 89-metre-long cylinder of rotary kiln 7.

Abkühlung des Klinkers im Planetenkühler auf etwa 130 Grad Celsius

The clinker is cooled to about 130 °C in the satellite cooling system.

Der Brennstand bildet den Endpunkt der linear angeordneten Zementofenanlage.

The linear cement-kiln complex is terminated by the "fireman's stand".

where, at a temperature of about 1,450 °C, it is heated almost to the point of fusion. The chemical and mineral transformation the material undergoes in the process of sintering produces a grey-black, coarse-grain cement clinker. The material leaves the firing zone in the 89-metre-long rotary kiln and falls into a satellite cooling system, comprising ten tubes, where its temperature is reduced to about 130 °C.

The fuels used to generate these high temperatures are coal, oil, natural gas, recycling oil and old tyres. The scope for flexibility in the firing process is demonstrated by the various ancillary structures around the heat-exchange tower, which have changed the original appearance of the tower to a large extent. After the cooling stage, the cement clinker is stored temporarily in six cylindrical silos with a total capacity of 110,000 tonnes.

Together with the cement silos and the dispatch area, the installations for the storage and processing of the cement clinker occupy the entire northern section of the site today. In the course of time, the historical railway station has become part of the industrial landscape.

In manufacturing Portland cement, cement clinker is pulverized with gypsum – added to control the setting property – in the cement mill. In manufacturing special types of cement, additives are substituted for part of the clinker before the pulverizing process. The fine cement powder is then sorted according to type and strength-grading and stored in 24 silos with a total capacity of 37,500 tonnes.

Vor der weiteren Verarbeitung wird der Klinker in sechs runden Silos aus Sichtbeton gelagert.

Before undergoing further processing, the clinker is stored in six cylindrical exposed-concrete silos.

Die Anlagen zur Lagerung und Verarbeitung des Zementklinkers nehmen zusammen mit den Zementsilos und den Versandeinrichtungen heute den gesamten Nordteil des Werksgeländes ein. Im Laufe der Zeit ist der historische Bahnhof zu einem Teil der Industrielandschaft geworden.

Zur Herstellung von Portlandzementen wird Zementklinker zusammen mit Gips (zur Steuerung der Abbindezeit) in der Zementmühle fein gemahlen. Bei besonderen Zementen wird vor dem Mahlvorgang ein Teil des Klinkers durch Zusätze ausgetauscht. Der gemahlene Zement wird dann, nach Sorten und Festigkeitsklassen getrennt, in 24 Silos mit einer Gesamtkapazität von 37.500 Tonnen gelagert.

Im Laufe der Entwicklung des Märkerwerks ist der historische Bahnhof von Harburg zu einem Teil der Industrielandschaft geworden.

In the course of its development, the Märker works has absorbed the historical railway station of Harburg, which now forms part of the industrial landscape.

Aus den Silos gelangt der Klinker in die Zementmühle. Hier wird er zusammen mit Gips zur Herstellung von Portlandzementen fein gemahlen.

The clinker is transferred from the silos to the cement mill, where it is mixed with gypsum and ground to a fine consistency to produce Portland cement.

The group of clinker silos – originally four in number, later extended to six – was also the outcome of a process in which various alternatives were explored. In the first planning stage, the requisite storage capacity of 70,000 tonnes was to be accommodated in a single large silo. The building form implied by this volume would have resulted in high costs for the design and implementation of the structure. What is more, the enormous mass of the building would have been completely out of scale.

Kurt Ackermann, therefore, appealed to the client to have the plant articulated into a number of elements: "By dividing it up into smaller silos, we sought solutions that would provide a structural and economical alternative. The series of studies we carried out also showed quite clearly that the construction costs were linked to the ratio of diameter to height.

Through the phased use of sliding shuttering, an optimum construction period and a high degree of economic efficiency were achieved. The access core, occupying a central position and designed as a light steel framework in a transparent form of construction, accommodates the bucket conveyor system, a staircase and lifts."

Viewed from the main road, the group of silos bears striking witness to the economic strength of the concern.

Auch die Gruppe der ursprünglich vier, später auf sechs erweiterten Klinkersilos ist das Ergebnis einer alternativen Untersuchung. In der ersten Planungsstufe war die notwendige Lagerkapazität von 70.000 Tonnen zunächst in einem Großsilo vorgesehen. Die aus dem Volumen sich ergebende Gebäudeform führte jedoch zu hohen Aufwendungen für die konstruktive Durchbildung. Außerdem hätte eine solche enorme Baumasse jeden Maßstab gesprengt.

Deshalb setzte sich Kurt Ackermann beim Bauherrn für eine Gliederung der Anlage ein: »Durch die Aufteilung in kleinere Silos suchten wir nach Lösungen, die eine konstruktive und wirtschaftliche Alternative darstellten. Die Untersuchungsreihe ergab auch hier deutlich die Abhängigkeit von Durchmesser und Höhe zu den Herstellungskosten. Durch den Einsatz von Gleitschalungen im Taktverfahren wurden günstige Bauzeiten und eine gute Wirtschaftlichkeit erreicht. Zentral ist der Erschließungskern angeordnet und als Gerüst in leichter, transparenter Stahlkonstruktion für die Becherwerke, Treppen und Aufzüge ausgebildet.«

Besonders von der Bundesstraße aus gesehen ist die Silogruppe ein markantes Zeugnis für die Leistungskraft des Unternehmens.

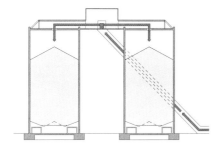

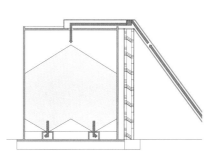

Schnitte durch die Planungsalternative von Silogruppe und großem Einzelsilo

Alternative planning proposals: sections through group of silos, and through single, large-scale silo

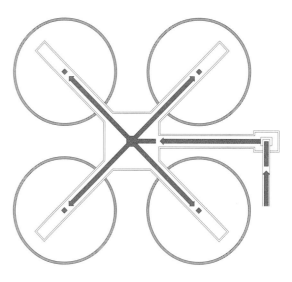

Die Gruppe der ursprünglich vier runden Klinkersilos wurde später auf sechs erweitert.

The original group of four cylindrical clinker silos was later extended to six.

Vor dem Versand wird der gemahlene Zement, nach Sorten und Festigkeitsklassen getrennt, in 24 Silos mit einer Gesamtkapazität von 37.500 Tonnen gelagert.

Prior to dispatch, the ground cement is sorted into different types and strengths and stored in 24 silos with a total capacity of 37,500 tonnes.

Like all other operational units, the workshops have changed considerably over the years. The first new workshop building was erected in 1963–64 and was closely linked – in time and location – to the homogenization plant project. In contrast to the tall group of silos, the workshops were constructed as a low-rise complex in reinforced concrete, with precast concrete columns and prestessed girders. The roof was covered with aerated concrete slabs with a felt-and-gravel finish. To emphasize the close links with the works' own production, the infill wall panels were executed in sandlime bricks. In addition to the workshops, the building accommodates the ancillary stores.

Ultimately, with the expansion of the Märker works, the building was no longer able to meet the requirements. Sections of the workshops and stores were, therefore, relocated; but the scattering of these facilities meant that the cogent spatial and functional relationships in the workshop area were lost.

Die neuen Werkstätten liegen im Zentrum des Werksgeländes. Ein Hochregallager überragt die zwischen 1992 und 1996 errichtete, kammartig gegliederte Anlage.

The new workshops, with a comb-like layout, were erected between 1992 and 1996 and occupy a central position on the works site. Rising above them at the back is the high-bay warehouse.

Wie alle anderen Betriebsteile haben sich auch die Werkstätten im Laufe der Jahrzehnte erheblich gewandelt. Das erste neue Werkstattgebäude entstand 1963/64 in zeitlicher und räumlicher Verbindung mit dem Projekt der Homogenisierungsanlage. Der im Unterschied zur hohen Silogruppe ausgeprägte Flachbau wurde aus Stahlbetonelementen mit vorgefertigten Stützen und vorgespannten Bindern konstruiert, mit Gasbetonplatten abgedeckt und mit einem Kiespressdach versehen. Zur Ausfachung der Wände wurden, um die Nähe zur werkseigenen Produktion zu betonen, Kalksandsteine verwendet. Neben den Werkstätten waren im Gebäude die zugeordneten Magazine untergebracht.

Aufgrund der Expansion des Märkerwerks konnte das Gebäude den Anforderungen schließlich nicht mehr genügen. Deshalb mussten Teile der Werkstätten und Magazine ausgelagert werden. Durch die immer dezentraleren Standorte ging jedoch nicht nur der räumliche, sondern auch der funktionale Zusammenhang im Werkstattbereich verloren.

Since maintenance and repair work within the plant has to be carried out quickly, efficiently and rationally, the construction of a new central workshop building with an adjoining high-bay warehouse was a necessary and logical step. The new facilities were completed in 1996. The comb-like layout ensured ideal functional links, short routes and a clear sense of orientation within the building.

The high-bay warehouse forms the spine of the layout, occupying the space north of the lime works. The four "teeth" of the comb house two metalworking shops with a training workshop; a workshop for quarry equipment; and one for the electrical department. The various areas are linked by an internal route. While the load-bearing structure reflects the functions performed in this tract, the outward appearance expresses a clear technical aesthetic, the shallow-pitched roofs accentuating the independent nature of this group of buildings within the works as a whole.

Eine technische Ästhetik prägt das Erscheinungs-bild der Werkstätten. Die flachen Satteldächer betonen die Eigenstän-digkeit der Baugruppe.

The workshops are distinguished by their clear technical aesthetic. The shallow-pitched roofs accentuate the independent nature of this tract.

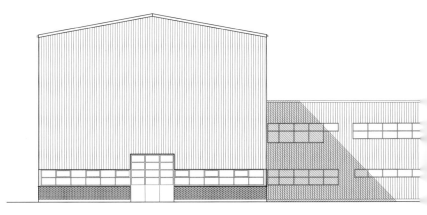

Weil der Wartungs- und Reparaturbereich im Werk nach Schnelligkeit, Effizienz und Rationalität verlangt, war der 1996 fertig gestellte Neubau von zentralen Werkstätten mit angeschlossenem Hochregallager eine notwendige und folgerichtige Lösung. Die kammartige Organisation des Grundrisses führte zu optimalen Funktionszusammenhängen, kurzen Wegen und einer guten Orientierung im Gebäude.

Der Baukörper des Hochregallagers bildet das Rückgrat der Anlage, die den Raum nördlich des Kalkwerks einnimmt. In den vier ›Fingern‹ sind zwei Schlossereien mit Lehrwerkstatt und je eine Werkstatt für die Steinbruchgeräte und für die Elektroabteilung untergebracht. Alle Bereiche werden durch die innere Werkstattstraße erschlossen. Die Tragwerke sind auf die Nutzung ausgerichtet. Das Erscheinungsbild wird durch eine klare technische Ästhetik geprägt, wobei die flach geneigten Satteldächer die Eigenständigkeit der Baugruppe im Werk betonen.

Reparaturwerkstatt für Schwerlastkipper des Steinbruchs. Außenansicht auf der linken Seite

Repair workshop for heavy-duty dumper trucks used in the quarry. Opposite page: external view

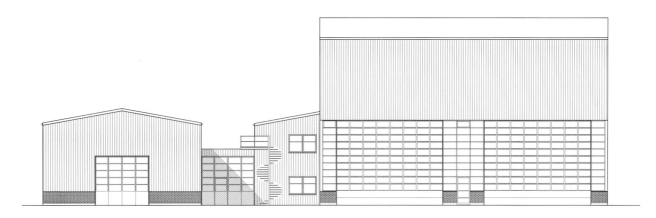

For more than 110 years, the Märker works has been a major employer in the region between Donauwörth and Nördlingen. In spite of increasing mechanization and rationalization, this medium-sized family concern has not only maintained the number of its employees, but has, in fact, enlarged it to a staff of more than 360 persons.

Many employees come from families that have worked for the company for three generations; and most individuals of the staff received their training at the works. More individuals have been trained at Märker during the past 30 years than the number of employees working for the company today. At present, some 40 trainees are acquiring professional qualifications in the workshops, in the laboratory and in the administration.

The new workshops provide a good example of the social responsibility assumed by the firm: in the clear articulation of the plant, in the generous spatial dimensions, and in the technical facilities and the carefully planned daylighting of the working areas. Long strip windows with clearly defined opening lights, and fully glazed wall bays provide every workplace with the requisite degree of natural light and ventilation. Inserted within this tract is the cubic volume of the cafeteria, which opens on to the surroundings in the form of room-height glazing on three sides. Landscaped courtyards between the teeth of the comb create a controlled transition to the works site.

Nowhere is the purpose of the buildings concealed, though. On the contrary, the range of materials specified – from clear glass and translucent elements to the brightly gleaming ribbed metal sheeting – aptly reflects the technical character of the complex.

Alle Räume der Werkstätten sind großzügig dimensioniert: oben das Halbzeuglager, unten eine Schlosserei.

All workshop spaces are generously dimensioned; above: the store for semi-finished products; below: a metal-working shop.

Durch voll verglaste
Wandfelder wird auch
die Elektrowerkstatt
natürlich belichtet.

Natural lighting of the
electrical workshop is
facilitated by fully
glazed wall bays.

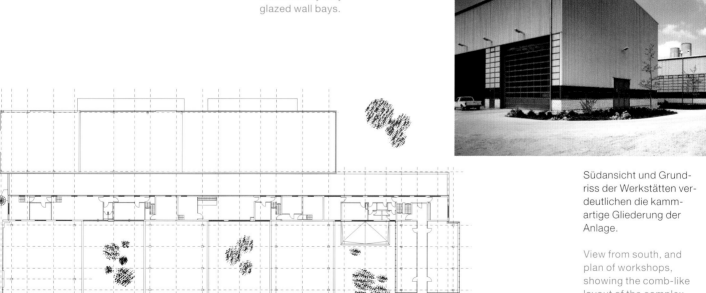

Südansicht und Grund-
riss der Werkstätten ver-
deutlichen die kamm-
artige Gliederung der
Anlage.

View from south, and
plan of workshops,
showing the comb-like
layout of the complex

77

Begrünte Höfe zwischen den Kammbauten bilden einen gestalteten Übergang zum Werksgelände. Im Hintergrund der eingestellte Kubus der Cafeteria

Landscaped courtyards between the teeth of the workshop "comb" form a controlled transition to the works site. In the background, the cubic volume of the cafeteria can be seen.

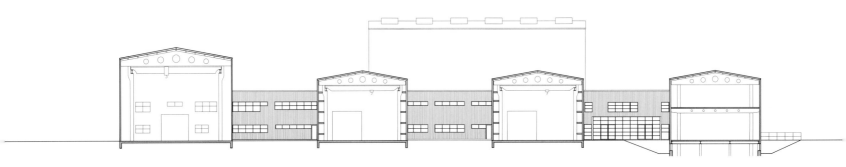

Querschnitt der Kammbauten: Die Tragwerke der Hallen sind eindeutig auf die Nutzung ausgerichtet.

Cross-section through the comb-like tracts of the workshop complex: the load-bearing structure of the halls is clearly based on functional needs.

Seit über 110 Jahren ist das Märkerwerk ein bedeutender Arbeit-
geber der Region zwischen Donauwörth und Nördlingen. Trotz
zunehmender Mechanisierung
und Rationalisierung ist es dem
mittelständischen Familienunternehmen gelungen, den Personal-
stand nicht nur zu halten, sondern
auf nunmehr über 360 Beschäf-
tigte auszubauen.

Viele Mitarbeiter sind bereits in
der dritten Familiengeneration im
Werk tätig. Dabei hat der größte
Teil der Beschäftigten eine Ausbildung im Unternehmen selbst er-
halten – während der letzten
dreißig Jahre wurden mehr Mitarbeiter ausgebildet als die Beleg-
schaft heute zählt. Derzeit erwer-
ben in den Werkstätten, im Labor
und in der Verwaltung rund 40
Auszubildende ihre berufliche
Qualifikation.

Die soziale Verantwortung der
Firma drückt sich gerade in den
neuen Werkstätten beispielhaft
aus: in der übersichtlichen Gliederung der Anlage, in den groß-
zügigen Dimensionen der Räume
sowie in der technischen Ausstat-
tung und präzisen Belichtung der
Arbeitsflächen. Lange Fenster-
bänder mit ablesbar eingesetzten
Öffnungsflügeln oder voll verglaste Wandfelder versorgen jeden
Arbeitsplatz mit dem notwendigen
Tageslicht und natürlicher Belüf-
tung. Auf drei Seiten raumhoch
verglast, öffnet sich auch der
eingestellte Kubus der Cafeteria
zur Umgebung. Begrünte Höfe
zwischen den Kammbauten bilden
einen gestalteten Übergang zum
Werksgelände.

Dabei wird der Zweck der
baulichen Anlage nirgendwo
kaschiert. Im Gegenteil: Durch
den Materialkanon von Klarglas,
transluzenten Elementen und
dem hell schimmernden Trapezblech tritt der technische Charakter des Bauwerks angemessen
in Erscheinung.

Auf drei Seiten raum-
hoch verglast, öffnet
sich auch der lichterfüll-
te Kubus der Cafeteria
zur Umgebung.

With full-height glazing
on three sides, the cubic
volume of the cafeteria
is filled with light and
open to the surround-
ings.

The story returns to its starting point. With the circular mixing bed, taken into operation in the autumn of 2000, the cycle of constructional refurbishment and extension of the Märker works has reached its conclusion for the present. The latest development is located to the south of the factory complex exactly on the spot where the Titan crushing plant for the cement works was erected in the late 1950s. This crushing plant was the first development undertaken by Ackermann und Partner in what was to become a long process of planning for the works. In the course of this collaboration, the architects were able to count on the co-operation of the company engineers at all time.

The circular mixing bed, which operates according to the "Chevron method", has the function of supplying the raw mill with material of a more homogeneous quality. This, in turn, ensures that the rotary kiln is fed with raw meal of a more uniform consistency. Emissions from the kiln should also be reduced in the process.

The raw material is transported to the circular mixing bed via an elevated conveyor belt connected to the new transfer station in the existing strip that runs north to the linear mixing bed. This bridge-like structure, supported on two columns and suspended from the centre of the roof over the mixing bed, conveys the material to the stacker. The homogenized raw material is removed by means of rakes and bridge scrapers, initially to the centre of the mixing bed, then subsequently through a tunnel to the new eastern transfer station in the conveyor strip leading to the raw mill.

In planning the circular mixing bed, the architects were confronted with the task of designing a plant that would, first and foremost, protect the surrounding areas from noise pollution. To meet these conditions in an optimum manner, an unconventional form of construction was chosen. A circle of 16 self-supporting, curved, triangular-section lattice girders form a vaulted, dome-like space that provides adequate headroom over the plant beneath.

The girders consist of tubular members and are anchored at their feet in massive reinforced concrete foundations. At the centre of this steel structure, which has a clear span of 106 metres, the girders are connected to a compression tie ring from which the material delivery station is also suspended.

The load-bearing steel structure was to remain visible. Fixing plates were, therefore, welded to the lower chords of the girders, thus enabling the membrane roof to be attached to the underside of the structure. The membrane is capable of bearing tensile loads. By drawing up the radial "ridge" cables at regular intervals, the skin acquired its characteristic wave-like form beneath the girders. An equally important distinguishing feature of the translucent roof skin is its double-curved, saddle-shaped surface. This is formed by radial valley cables spanned over the top of the membrane half-way between the girders. The cables allow the material to be stressed. The ten-sile stresses in the cables themselves are transmitted to massive foundations anchored in the ground.

At its lower edge, the membrane is reinforced by a cable welded into a peripheral seam. The curved form adopted by this cable reflects the specific stress conditions along the edge. At the bottom of each half bay, therefore, there is an arched opening with a clear headroom of about four metres in the middle through which lorries and large plant can pass. Below the compression ring at the crest of the dome is an internal flat steel ring to which the upper edge of the membrane is clamped and to which the 16 radial ridge cables and 17 valley cables are fixed.

The striking large-scale form of the 32-metre-high circular mixing bed might be regarded as a celebratory dome for the raw materials limestone and clay. The appearance of the Märker complex is thus enriched by a further design element – a structure with a technical aesthetic that is again derived from the form of construction and the function it has to fulfil.

Das neue Rundmisch-
bett dominiert seit
Herbst 2000 das südli-
che Werksgelände. Die
transluzente Dachhaut
wurde unterhalb des
Tragwerks befestigt, um
die Stahlkonstruktion
nicht zu verhüllen.
Die Stahlkonstruktion
aus Dreigurtbindern hat
eine Spannweite von
106 Metern.

The new circular mixing
bed, taken into opera-
tion in the autumn of
2000, now dominates
the southern part of the
site. In order not to con-
ceal the steel structure,
the translucent roof skin
was attached to the
underside. The steel
structure, consisting
of triangular-section
lattice girders, spans a
distance of 106 metres.

Zurück zum Ausgangspunkt: Mit
dem im Herbst 2000 fertig gestellten Rundmischbett hat sich im
Märkerwerk der Kreis von bauli-
cher Sanierung und Erweiterung
vorerst geschlossen. Die neueste
Anlage nimmt nämlich im Süden
des Fabrikgeländes genau jenen
Ort ein, an dem in den späten
fünfziger Jahren der Titanbrecher
des Zementwerks errichtet worden war. Dieser Brecher war die
erste Maßnahme im Rahmen der
langfristigen Werksplanung von
Ackermann und Partner, bei der
die Architekten auch stets auf die
Kooperationsbereitschaft der Be-
triebsingenieure zählen konnten.

Das nach der ›Chevron-Me-
thode‹ betriebene Rundmischbett
hat die Funktion, das Rohmaterial
mit einem höheren Grad an Ho-
mogenität der Rohmühle und somit das Rohmehl gleichmäßiger
als bisher dem Brennprozess im
Zementofen zuzuführen. Dadurch
sollen im Bereich des Drehofens
auch niedrigere Emissionen erreicht werden.

Das Rundmischbett erhält das
Rohmaterial über eine Bandbrücke, die mit der neuen Übergabestation im schon lange beste-
henden, nördlich verlaufenden
Förderband zum Längsmischbett
verbunden ist. Diese auf zwei
Stützen aufgelagerte und vom
Zentrum des Rundmischbetts ab-
gehängte Bandbrücke übergibt
das Material dem Absetzer. Der
Abtransport des homogenisierten
Rohstoffs erfolgt über Rechen und
Kratzkettenförderer zunächst zum
Mittelpunkt des Mischbetts und
anschließend durch einen Tunnel
zur neuen östlichen Übergabestation auf die Bandstraße zur
Rohmühle.

Bei der Planung des Rundmischbetts standen die Architekten vor
der Aufgabe, eine Anlage zu ent-
wickeln, die in erster Linie die
Umwelt vor Schallemissionen
schützt. Um diese Randbedin-
gung optimal erfüllen zu können,
wurde eine unkonventionelle Konstruktion gewählt.

16 bogenförmig gekrümmte
Dreigurtbinder aus Rundrohren,
die an ihren Fußpunkten auf mas-
siven Stahlbetonfundamenten
aufgelagert sind, überspannen
freitragend das Lichtraumprofil
der Maschine. Im Zentrum der
Stahlkonstruktion, deren Spannweite 106 Meter beträgt, sind diese Binder durch einen Druckring
miteinander verbunden, an dem
zugleich die Abwurfstation ab-
gehängt ist.

Um die tragende Stahlkon-
struktion nicht zu verhüllen, wurden an den Untergurten der Binder Laschen angeschweißt, die es
ermöglicht haben, die eigentliche
Dachhaut in Form einer konstruktiven Membran zu befestigen.
Durch das punktuelle Hochziehen
der Firstseile ergab sich die cha-
rakteristische Wellenform der

Membran unterhalb der Binder.
Mindestens ebenso prägend für
die Erscheinung der transluzenten
Dachhaut sind die sattelförmigen,
zweifach gekrümmten Flächen:
Sie wurden erzeugt durch ›Kehlseile‹, die jeweils zwischen den

Bindern über der Membran angeordnet sind und eine Belastbarkeit
des zugfesten Materials erlauben.
Die in diesen Seilen herrschenden
Zugspannungen werden am Boden von Schwergewichtsfunda-
menten aufgenommen.

Der untere Membranrand ist
mit einem eingeschweißten Rand-
seil verstärkt und entsprechend
den spezifischen Spannungsver-
hältnissen so gekrümmt, dass im
mittleren Bereich allseitig eine
Durchfahrtshöhe von rund vier
Metern für Lastwagen und Groß-
geräte gegeben ist. Der obere
Membranabschluss wird durch einen innen liegenden, unter dem
Druckring angebrachten Flach-
stahlring gebildet, an dem zum
einen die Membran angeklemmt
ist und zum anderen die 16 Firstseile sowie die 17 Kehlseile ange-
schlossen wurden.

Die markante Großform des
32 Meter hohen Rundmischbetts
lässt sich gleichsam als ›Dom‹ für
die Rohstoffe Kalkstein und Ton
begreifen. Durch diese Anlage
wurde das Erscheinungsbild des
Märkerwerks um ein neues gestal-
terisches Element bereichert, das

wiederum im Sinne technischer
Ästhetik ganz aus der Funktion
und Konstruktion entstanden ist.

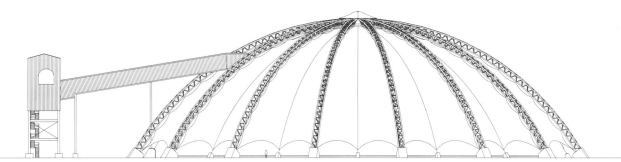

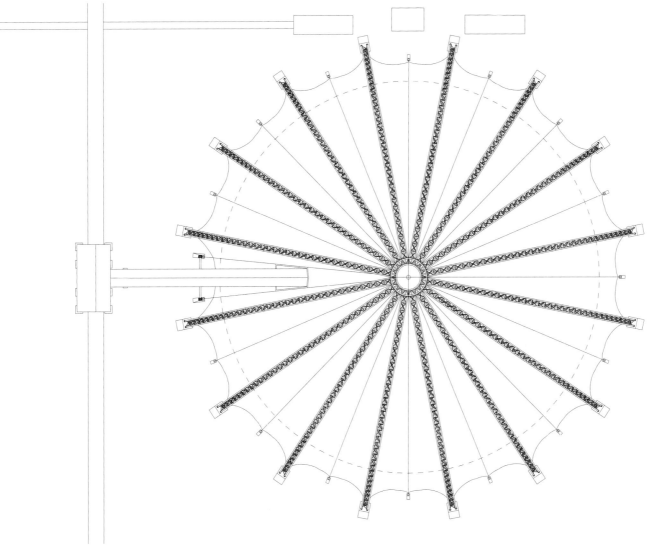

The Poetry of Functionalism

The Märker works' construction programme that has continued now for more than 40 years is probably unique in Europe. Despite extensive investigations, it was not possible to find a comparable example in the field of industrial building of a client refurbishing and extending his concern in one location and over such a long period of time in collaboration with a single architectural team. Here, far more than in other comparable cases, one can legitimately pay tribute to the joint achievement of client and architect.

The ongoing development of the Märker works is a success story that can be measured not only in terms of time, however, but economically and in the context of industrial operations and design. Through the constant process of renewal of the plant and the extended range of products, the company has established a sound economic basis. Secondly, large-scale investments have led to a fundamental improvement in working condi-

tions. Large-scale equipment, machinery and automatic plant - used in all areas from the quarry to the dispatch department – have gradually come to replace the heavy, dirty manual labour of former times and have helped to reduce night and weekend shift work as well. Thirdly, the enormous progress made in dust-removal technology has greatly improved the environmental quality, both within the works and in the surrounding areas.

Mention should be made of one particularly fortunate aspect, namely the design of the buildings, which manifests itself in the distinguished appearance of the plant. The client's commitment to this cause has meant that he was never in danger of confusing "economy" with "cheapness". This enabled the architects Ackermann und Partner to design functionally appropriate buildings with constructional intelligence and in a technically beautiful form

– removed from all those architectural fashions that, over the past decades, have had such a negative influence even on industrial construction. Last, but not least, as Richard Martin, the long-year project architect for the Märker works, observes, this joint success story was attributable to an ongoing co-operation with building contractors who proved to be close and reliable partners in the execution of the concrete and steel structures.

As early as 1923, the architectural critic Adolf Behne formulated an idea in the now classical words that might aptly be applied to the Märker works, remarking that "returning to function always has a revolutionizing effect: forms that have grown tyrannical are cast off, and in contemplating the original purpose from as neutral a standpoint as possible, a rejuvenated, living, breathing form is created". In this way, it is possible to attain that poetry of functionalism which allows industrial building to be recognized as a cultural achievement.

Poesie der Sachlichkeit

Linke Seite: Grundriss
des Rundmischbetts.
Unten: Blick durch den
32 Meter hohen Hallen-
raum mit der zentral an-
geordneten Maschine.

Opposite page: plan of
circular mixing bed.
Below: view through the
32-metre-high dome-
like space with the plant
located in the middle

Das nunmehr über vierzigjährige Bauen am Märkerwerk ist in Europa wohl einzigartig. Trotz intensiver Recherchen ließ sich im Bereich des Industriebaus kein zweites Beispiel dafür finden, dass ein Bauherr zusammen mit nur einem Architektenteam über einen derart langen Zeitraum hinweg sein Unternehmen an einem Ort saniert und erweitert hat. Weit mehr als in anderen Fällen ist es hier legitim, die gemeinsame Leistung von Bauherr und Architekt herauszustellen.

Aber nicht nur zeitlich, sondern auch ökonomisch, betrieblich und gestalterisch stellt die kontinuierliche Entwicklung des Märkerwerks eine Erfolgsgeschichte dar. Erstens steht das Unternehmen durch seine ständig erneuerten Anlagen und seine erweiterte Produktpalette auf einer wirtschaftlich gesunden Grundlage. Zum zweiten wurden durch die umfangreichen Investitionen die Arbeitsverhältnisse grundlegend verbessert: Der Einsatz von Großgeräten, Maschinen und automatischen Anlagen hat – vom Steinbruch bis hin zum Versand – schrittweise die ehemals schwere und schmutzige Handarbeit abgelöst, außerdem Nacht- und Wochenendschichten reduziert. Zum dritten hat durch die immensen Fortschritte in der Entstaubungstechnologie die Umwelt mehr Qualität gewonnen, sowohl innerhalb des Werks als auch außerhalb.

Einen Glücksfall darf man aber nennen, dass sich das Unternehmen auch durch die Gestalt seiner Bauten anspruchsvoll präsentiert. Der Bauherr war durch sein Engagement davor gefeit, ›wirtschaftlich‹ mit ›billig‹ zu verwechseln. Dies gab den Architekten Ackermann und Partner die Möglichkeit, das funktional Richtige mit konstruktiver Intelligenz im technisch Schönen zum Ausdruck zu bringen – abseits aller Architekturmoden, die während der letzten Jahrzehnte sogar den Industriebau negativ beeinflusst haben. Nicht zuletzt hat zum gemeinsamen Erfolg ein Umstand beigetragen, auf den Richard Martin, der langjährige Projektarchitekt für das Märkerwerk, mit Bedacht hinweist: die Kontinuität der ausführenden Firmen, die im Betonbau wie im Stahlbau vertraute und verlässliche Partner waren.

Was das Erscheinungsbild des Märkerwerks verkörpert, hat der Architekturkritiker Adolf Behne bereits 1923 in die klassischen Worte gefasst: »Das Zurückgehen auf den Zweck wirkt also immer wieder revolutionierend, wirft tyrannisch gewordene Formen ab, um aus der Besinnung auf die ursprüngliche Funktion aus einem möglichst neutralen Zustand eine verjüngte, lebendige, atmende Form zu schaffen.« So kann jene Poesie der Sachlichkeit entstehen, die den Industriebau als eine Kulturleistung vor Augen führt.

Das Unternehmen Chronologie des Märkerwerks	1889	Gründung eines Stein- und Kalkwerks durch August Märker in Harburg	August Märker founds a stone and lime works in Harburg.
The concern A chronology of the Märker works	1892	Einrichtung einer Dampfziegelei	Installation of a steam-operated brickworks
	1901	Bau eines Kalkringofens und eines Schotterwerks	Construction of a circular lime kiln and a stone-crushing plant
	1906	Aufnahme der Zementproduktion, Stillegung der Dampfziegelei. Änderung des Firmennamens in »Portlandzement-Fabrik, Stein- und Kalkwerk August Märker«	Start of cement production; closure of the steam-operated brickworks. The company changes its name to "August Märker Portland Cement Factory, Stone and Lime Works"
	1908	Großbrand mit teilweiser Zerstörung der Werksanlagen. Wiederaufbau der Zementfabrik	A conflagration destroys part of the works. Reconstruction of the cement factory
	1909	Umwandlung des bisherigen Einzelunternehmens in eine GmbH	Conversion of the single-owner firm into a limited liability company
	1948	Neugründung der »Schwäbische Kalkwerk GmbH«	Founding of Schwäbische Kalkwerk GmbH (Swabian Lime Works)
	1958	Beginn der langfristigen Werks-planung mit den Architekten Ackermann und Partner	Commencement of long-term planning of works in collaboration with the architects Ackermann und Partner
	1960	Namensänderung von »Portland-zement-Fabrik August Märker GmbH« in »Märker Zementwerk GmbH«	Name changed from August Märker Portland Cement Factory to Märker Cement Works (Märker Zementwerk GmbH)
	1963	Umstellung von Nass- auf Trockenverfahren	Change from wet to dry production process
	1973	Inbetriebnahme des Wärmetauscher-Drehofens 7	Heat-exchange rotary kiln 7 taken into operation
	1979	Inbetriebnahme des Kalkschacht-ofens III für Öl und Gas	Lime shaft kiln III taken into operation; run on oil and gas
	1980	Gründung der »Märker Transport-beton GmbH«	Founding of Märker Transportbeton GmbH (ready-mixed conrete company)
	1981	Gründung der »Märker Land- und Forstwirtschaft GbR«	Founding of Märker Land- und Forstwirschaft GbR (agricultural and forestry company)
	1986	Inbetriebnahme des Kalkschacht-ofens IV für Kohle und Gas	Lime shaft kiln IV taken into operation; run on coal and gas
	1989	Hundertjähriges Firmenjubiläum	100th anniversary of founding of company
	1992	Gründung der »Märker Umwelttechnik GmbH«	Founding of Märker Umwelttechnik GmbH (environmental technology company)
	1994	Gründung der »Märker Holding GmbH«	Founding of Märker Holding GmbH
	1995	Berufung von Dr. Wolfgang Märker zum Vorsitzenden des Beirats der »Märker Holding GmbH«	Dr Wolfgang Märker appointed chairman of advisory board of Märker Holding GmbH
	2000	Fertigstellung des Rundmischbetts	Completion of circular mixing bed

Entwurf, Planung, Bauleitung/ Design, planning, site management	Ackermann und Partner Architekten BDA Malsenstraße 57 80638 München/Munich Professor Dr. techn. Kurt Ackermann Dipl. Ing. Peter Ackermann	

Partner/Partners:
Ing. grad. Richard Martin bis/until 1997
Dipl. Ing. Jürgen Feit bis/until 1980

Mitarbeiter/Assistants:
Horst Raab
Dieter Kiermaier
Roland Rieger
Heinz Riegel
Jens Viehweg
Eoin Bowler
Richard Fischer
Dieter Raab
Martin Reinfelder
Heinz Hirschhäuser

Tragwerksplanung/
Structural
engineering

Dipl. Ing. Friedrich Brosch
Alexander Brosch
München/Munich

Mitarbeiter/Assistants:
Dipl. Ing. Ernst Braun
Dipl. Ing. Walter Bernd

Dipl. Ing. Albrecht Noller
Hochtief Fertigteilbau

Fichtner + Köppl
Rosenheim
Dr.-Ing. Johann Köppl

Prüfstatik/
Proof engineers

Landesgewerbeanstalt LGA
Augsburg

Landschafts-
gestaltung/
Landscape design

Professor Karl Kagerer
Landschaftsarchitekt/
Landscapearchitect
Ismaning

Ellen Märker
Harburg

Diese Publikation wurde unterstützt
von folgenden Firmen/
This publication was supported by
the following companies:

Arlt Bauunternehmung GmbH, Nördlingen
Birdair Europe Stromeyer GmbH, Konstanz
Maschinenfabrik Bernhard Beumer KG, Beckum
DBT Mineral Processing GmbH & Co. KG, Lünen
Dyckerhoff + Widmann AG, Augsburg
Egner GmbH, Reimlingen
Eigner Fertigbau GmbH & Co. KG, Nördlingen
Eisenbau Weißenburg GmbH & Co., Weißenburg
Fichtner + Köppl Statik, Rosenheim
F. L. Smidth & Co. A/S, Valby, Kopenhagen/Copenhagen
Karl Glock GmbH, Metallbau, Donauwörth
Haver & Boecker Maschinenfabrik, Oelde
Hans Herold GmbH, Augsburg
Hochtief Fertigteilbau GmbH, Königsbrunn
HPC Harress Pickel Consult GmbH, Harburg
Franz Leinfelder Logistik GmbH, Wemding
Loesche GmbH, Düsseldorf
Lurgi Lentjes Service GmbH, Frankfurt
Maerz Ofenbau GmbH, Düsseldorf
Maurer Söhne GmbH & Co. KG, München/Munich
MC-Bauchemie, Bochum
Siemens AG, Augsburg
Svedala Deutschland GmbH, Ketsch
Schwenck Process GmbH, Darmstadt
Alois Scheuch GmbH, Ried
Schweihofer Gerüstbautechnik GmbH, Mertingen
Zeppelin Baumaschinen, Böblingen

Weiterführende Literatur / Selected Literature

Kurt Ackermann und Partner, Bauten und Projekte (1953 bis 1978), Stuttgart 1978.
Ackermann und Partner, Bauten und Projekte 1978–1998, Ingeborg Flagge (Hrsg.), Einführung von Wolfgang Jean Stock, München 1998.
Adolf Behne, Der moderne Zweckbau, Nachdruck der Originalausgabe von 1923, Vorwort von Ulrich Conrads, Bauwelt Fundamente, Bd. 10, Frankfurt/Main und Berlin 1964.
Sigfried Giedion, Bauen in Frankreich – Bauen in Eisen – Bauen in Eisenbeton, Nachdruck der Originalausgabe von 1928, Nachwort von Sokratis Georgiadis, Berlin 2000.
Walter Gropius, Die Entwicklung moderner Industriebaukunst, in: Jahrbuch des Deutschen Werkbundes, Jena 1913.
Gert Kähler, Pragmatisch, praktisch, gut. Neufert und die Industriearchitektur nach 1945, in: Walter Prigge (Hrsg.), Ernst Neufert, Normierte Baukultur, Frankfurt/Main und New York 1999.

Fotonachweis:
Alle Fotografien stammen von Hans Neudecker, Rotis,
mit folgenden Ausnahmen:
Archiv Märker, Harburg 7, 8, 9
Sigrid Neubert, München 10, 11, 12, 31, 48, 49, 51, 52, 53,
54, 55, 60, 61, 62
Jens Weber, München 75

Zeichnungen:
Florian Lechner, München

© Prestel Verlag, München · London · New York, 2000

Auf dem Umschlag: Märker Zementwerk Harburg
Foto: Hans Neudecker

Die Deutsche Bibliothek – CIP Einheitsaufnahme
Ein Titelsatz für diese Publikation ist bei der Deutschen
Bibliothek erhältlich

Prestel Verlag · Mandlstraße 26 · 80802 München
Tel. 089/381709-0 · Fax 089/381709-35
www.prestel.de

Lektorat: Katharina Wurm, München
Gestaltung: Hans Neudecker, Rotis
Herstellung: Rainald Schwarz, München
Reproduktionen: Peter Schamschula Reprotechnik,
Leutkirch
Druck und Bindung: Sellier, Freising

Gedruckt auf chlorfrei gebleichtem Papier

Printed in Germany
ISBN 3-7913-2402-0

Photocredits:
All photographs are by Hans Neudecker, Rotis,
with the following exceptions:
Märker Archive, Harburg 7, 8, 9
Sigrid Neubert, Munich 10, 11, 12, 31, 48, 49, 51, 52, 53,
54, 55, 60, 61, 62
Jens Weber, Munich 75

Drawings:
Florian Lechner, Munich

© Prestel Verlag, Munich · London · New York, 2000

Translated from the German by Peter Green

Cover: Märker Cement Works Harburg
Photo: Hans Neudecker

Library of Congress Cataloging-in-Publication Data
is available

Prestel Verlag
Mandlstaße 26 · 80802 Munich, Germany
Tel. +49 (89) 38 17 09-0 · Fax + 49 (89) 38 17 09-35;
175 5th Ave., Suite 402 · New York, NY 10010, USA
Tel. +1 (212) 995-2720, Fax +1 (212) 995-2733;
4 Bloomsbury Place · London WC1A 2QA, UK
Tel. +44 (020) 7323-5004 · Fax +44 (020) 7636-8004
www.prestel.com

Prestel books are available worldwide.
Please contact your nearest bookseller or write
to one of the above adresses for information
concerning your local distributor.

Editor: Katharina Wurm, Munich
Design: Hans Neudecker, Rotis
Production: Rainald Schwarz, Munich
Lithography: Peter Schamschula Reprotechnik, Leutkirch
Printing and Binding: Sellier, Freising

Printed in Germany
ISBN 3-7913-2402-0